ANYONE CAN START A BUSINESS

Stories compiled
by Barbie Ostler

Published by Zeosha, Inc
St George, UT USA

To my father and friend.
Brad Owen

Thank you for teaching
me what you know.

Copyright © 2024 by Barbie Ostler

All rights reserved. No part of this publication may be reproduced, distributed, or transmitted in any form or by any means, including photocopying, recording, or other electronic or mechanical methods, without the prior written permission of the publisher, except for brief quotations embodied in critical reviews and certain other noncommercial uses permitted by copyright law.

For permission requests, write to the publisher at Support@Zeosha.com, addressed "Permissions Department."

The author and publisher of this book do not dispense business advice but offer information of a general nature to help you in your quest for business success. This is not a step-by-step guide but an essence of inspiration.

This book is not intended as legal, business, accounting, or financial advice. You are advised to seek the services of competent professionals in these fields.

ISBN: Paperback: 978-1-963971-00-2,
Hardback: 978-1-963971-01-9,
Digital Online: 978-1-963971-02-6
Audio Book: 978-1-963971-03-3

About the Author

Barbie Ostler is a young aspiring entrepreneur who is deeply passionate about guiding others towards achieving their life goals. With a keen interest in practical business education, she has found a gap among her peers in choosing careers and knowing how to move their lives forward in business while still being able to enjoy the lives they live. She aims to fill it by showing that entrepreneurship is a valid choice through her book, "Anyone Can Start a Business."

Barbie's interest in entrepreneurship stems from her desire to help those of her and any generation realize there is more to life than getting "a job." It is important for her to understand life's purpose and enjoy the experience of living. Raised by an experienced entrepreneur, she cherishes the freedom that entrepreneurship brings and has observed the difference it can make in one's life. She believes that if people feel fulfilled in what they do, they will begin to see life as something to use and enjoy rather than run away from.

Leveraging her father's expertise as a seasoned entrepreneur, Barbie offers practical advice on starting and growing a business for young adults with minimal experience in entrepreneurship through thought-provoking yet simple questions. She wrote this book in Brad's voice since the stories and experiences are his.

Who is Brad Owen?

A Foreword by Barbie Ostler

Brad Owen is a genius. With an extensive professional journey spanning various industries, he has held significant positions and made meaningful contributions to science, technology, family, and community. Brad has provided valuable insights, drawing from years of experience across many career paths.

He has successfully started and operated multiple businesses, demonstrating adaptability across various industries. Brad Owen's history reflects a pragmatic and varied entrepreneurial journey. His portfolio spans ventures from a candy store and lawn care to less traditional endeavors such as dance instruction and wireless booster installation. He has engaged in real estate, investment training, and mortgage loans and even entered the digital realm with programming, internet marketing, and a YouTube channel. He tackled ventures including a salvage store and even motocross registration and tracking with a practical approach. He has been a senior radio frequency engineer and a microwave engineer, developing innovative solutions for spectrum management and enabling simultaneous operations for wireless phone carriers and existing incumbents and serving on the National Spectrum Management Association (NSMA) board in Washington, DC.

As chief science officer, he spearheaded research and development for an antimicrobial 1-micron clear coating. This groundbreaking project, with studies conducted at the University of Iowa, showcased its effectiveness in eliminating 99.9 percent of MRSA on surfaces used by hospital patients. In addition to roles in careers and starting businesses, Brad is actively involved in community service and leadership positions. His service on the boards of charter and private schools and the St. George Children's Museum as vice chair reflects Brad's commitment to community development.

However, what I find most inspiring about Brad Owen is his definition of success. Not by what he has accomplished but by what he learns from every new experience and venture and simply by who he is. "If I get out of bed every morning, that day is successful." He built himself into this man, growing his education independently rather than through a college or university. His kindness gives him an honor to know; his happiness makes him a pleasure to be around. He'll give you his thoughts exactly how he thinks them with no fluff. Success to him has little to do with the dollar made or the reach of a product, but what a blessing each new day is.

Barbie Ostler

How to Build Your Dream

An Introduction by Brad Owen

My name is Brad Owen. People have often asked me how to start a business or become successful. This book answers that question and many others I've been asked over the years. I'm so grateful for Barbie who saw value in my views and decided to write this book. I'm sharing these experiences to help inspire people who want more from their lives. The topics in this book are the basics of starting your own business: coming up with ideas, starting businesses, and finding new ways to make money while living the life you want.

Entrepreneurship is where your passions turn into realistic business ideas. Knowing what excites you is the starting point, guiding your journey and giving every decision a sense of purpose and drive. You don't have to be passionate about what you do if you're passionate about why you do it.

Successful businesses thrive by meeting a need, solving a problem, or filling a gap in the market. Figuring out this demand is crucial for building a great company. Long-lasting success comes from understanding why you're doing what you're doing. Knowing your core motivations will help you stay strong in tough times and thrive in the good ones.

In the chapters ahead, we'll explore picking the right business idea, understanding different markets, building your brand, calculating costs, finding funding, and learning from genuine business experiences. These insights will equip you with the tools and knowledge to drive your entrepreneurial dreams toward success. For ease of understanding, the book is sectioned into different steps in my business creation process.
The first section of the book consists of the chapters "I want to start a business, what do I do", through the chapter heading "How to find your

target market". These sections give a good grasp of how to get in the right mindset to work for yourself, how you can view the world more business focused, finding ideas everywhere, and the first few steps of how to set yourself up to begin your newfound ideas.

The second set of chapters primarily teach basic networking and marketing strategies. This is made up of the chapters "Networking", "Learning from your competition", "Branding", and "Marketing".

The following section is the longest, hitting on the technical side of turning a dream into a reality. If you don't keep track of how your business is doing correctly or where your income is going, you could lose what you built fast. This section are the chapters "Turning your idea into an opportunity" through "EIN Federal Tax ID" (Which is something you need when hiring employees, don't worry if it doesn't make sense now, it will once you get there)

Welcome to the realm of the entrepreneurial mindset—where dreams meet strategy, passion meets purpose, and innovation meets results.

Contents

About the Author iii
Who is Brad Owen? iv
How to Build Your Dream vi
I Want to Start a Business, What Do I Do? 1
    Looking at the World with New Eyes 1
    Seeing Opportunities 2
    Taking Opportunities 4
    Building Confidence 5
    Mindset Change: Money Is Everywhere 7
Kinds of Business 8
    What's Your "Why"? 9
    What Are You Passionate About? 10
    What Need Does Your Business Fill? 11
How to Choose an Idea 12
    Pick Your Passion 12
    Keep It Simple 13
    Scaling 14
Different Markets 16
    Saturated 16
    Dominated 17
    High Demand 18
    The Golden Ticket 18
How to Find Your Target Market 19
    What Kind of People Are You Marketing To? 19

- How Many People Want Your Product? 20
- Networking 22
  - Making Friends 22
  - People Just Like You 22
  - Sales Groups 23
  - Resourcing 23
  - Have Integrity 24
  - Networking for Introverts 25
- Learning from Your Competition 27
  - Pricing 28
  - Sales 28
  - Reviews 28
  - What If There Is No Competition? 29
- Branding 30
  - Choosing a Company Name 30
  - Colors, Style, and Fonts 31
  - Your Brand's Voice 32
- Marketing 34
  - Social Media Tips 35
- Turning Your Idea into an Opportunity 36
  - What Are You Selling? 36
  - How to Calculate Possible Costs 37
  - How to Markup Products and Why 38
  - Marking Up for Your Time 40
  - Mission Statement 42
  - Estimated Profits 42
- Investors, Rich Family, and Getting Money 44

- What's a Pitch?..44
- Working with Partners 44
- Family and Friends 50
- Angel Investors vs Opportunity Investors 50

Other Options for Money 52
- Stockholders 52
- Foundations 52
- Grants 52
- Partnering with a College 53
- Bootstrapping It 53

Raising Money 55
- Executive Summary...56
- Pitch Deck 56
- Prospectus...56
- Private Placement Memorandum 58

IPO and Private Funding 60
- Regulation A (Reg A)..60
- Regulation Crowdfunding (Reg CF) 61
- Regulation D (Reg D) 62
- Taking on a Business Partner 63

Licensing..64
- City License 65
- County License 66
- State License 66
- Home Occupation License 68
- Specialty Licenses...69

Legally a Business 70

- Sole Proprietor 70
- DBA 70
- C Corporation (C Corp) 71
- S Corporation (S Corp) 72
- Limited Liability Partnership (LLP) 72
- Limited Liability Company (LLC) 73
- Nonprofit Corporation 74
- B Corporation (Benefit Corporation) 75
- Close Corporation 75
- Business Insurance 76

Hiring an Accountant 78
- Schedule C 78
- PNL 79
- What Is a Fiscal Quarter? 80
- Balance Sheet 81
- 1099 Contractor 82

EIN Federal Tax ID 83
- Employees 84
- Hiring People 84

Extras 86
- Arrogance 86
- When to Hire People 86
- Processing Failure 87
- MLMs and Pyramid Schemes 90
- Scams and Dead Ends 91
- Door-to-Door Sales 93
- Affiliate Marketing 94

Final Thoughts 96
Notes 97

I Want to Start a Business, What Do I Do?

Looking at the World with New Eyes

When I was a young teen, I wanted to make money. I was out mowing my parent's lawn when I thought, "I wonder if my neighbors would pay me to do their lawn, too." I went door to door and asked my neighbors for a flat price of double the minimum wage to mow their lawns. If they wanted their yard trimmed as well, I would ask for quadruple the current minimum wage. I had a few neighbors that gave me money all summer! But then winter came, and it snowed a lot. I thought, "Oh no, there goes my business," until I realized people don't like shoveling their snow! And look at that! A new business was born! I asked if people would pay me to remove their snow through the winter. That business was much easier because I still charged double the minimum wage, but with a snow blower, it took me 15 minutes! I was able to make money all year. What I learned from this is you can make money just by asking.

Entrepreneurship isn't always about brilliant innovative ideas or life-changing business models. Most of the time, it's seeing a need and thinking, "I can do that." Changing how you see your daily life helps you notice chances for new things. You need to shift your thinking, worldview, and judgments about yourself and others to seize opportunity. When you start seeing and taking these opportunities, you'll be more open to trying new things and learning from them.

As embracing opportunities becomes a habit, you'll feel surer of yourself when facing the unknown and possible, or even probable, failure. This confidence comes from being okay with trying new things, knowing you've got what it takes to deal with whatever comes your way. Success is built from a life of persistent changes in perspective. It might sound cheesy, but if you believe in your abilities and ideas, you will help others believe in them and even buy them.

Seeing Opportunities

My journey to becoming a salvage store owner began when I moved to Georgia with my young family for a business opportunity. There, I witnessed the rise of a store that sold overstocked and returned items from other retailers at a low price. I learned this was a profitable and valuable business model, as many stores had excess inventory, they wanted to get rid of it quickly. Some items were brand new, while others were slightly used, but still functional. It was not the business opportunity I had moved for, but I was intrigued by this idea and decided to replicate it when I relocated to Seattle with my family. That's how I started B-Salvaged - a salvage store like the one I saw making money and filling a need in Georgia. It worked well, and there was definitely a market for it.

We started in November and ordered a full semi-truck of toys. Since everyone was buying toys for Christmas, we sold the entire truck in two weeks, which was super exciting! I got another full semi-truck and sold that one as well.

Then I bought two truckloads of something different because it was cheaper. I didn't realize the variety was limited to two items between the two trucks. That was terrible news. We were in a small town, and there was no way I would sell those two truckloads. The other problem is that people buy less in January than in November and December. In retail, you're at a loss until November. That is why they call it Black Friday. We managed to stay in business until our lease ran out in November. At that time, we had to decide whether to renew the lease or close the store. My family and I decided to close it. I learned to look for promising ideas and adapt them to fit new places and that keeping an eye on the market doesn't mean watching what's being sold at the time but what affects what I am selling, such as time of year and product. I also learned that cheaper doesn't mean better.

In this experience, you see both success and lack of foresight. If you start your own business, you will have many moments like this throughout your life. It is essential to change your plans according to the things you learn and what you see working.

Opportunities for entrepreneurship can arise from various sources and circumstances. Identifying unmet needs or gaps in the market lets you find innovative solutions. Keeping an eye on emerging technologies or advancements that could create new markets or disrupt existing ones is an excellent way to sneak in as new gaps are made apparent. Societal changes, shifts in consumer behavior, or evolving trends can create opportunities for new products or services. Anticipating and adapting to these changes leads to entrepreneurial ventures that can fill a need and be quite interesting for you. In short, opportunities are everywhere; you just need to learn how to see them.

This concept of opportunities being everywhere may seem great in theory, but you might be thinking, "Where do I start?" or "What does this have to do with me?" Think about the things you do every day. The items you use, the habits you've made. What would improve your daily experience? Your weekly experience? What do you wish you would have known as you learned how to navigate your everyday life? Do you remember the learning curves you went through? Could you monetize teaching people what you now know, or could you find a way to make it easier for others to do what you do daily?

By being observant, adaptable, and open-minded, entrepreneurs can identify and seize opportunities in various forms, leading to successful ventures that cater to evolving market needs or create entirely new markets.

Taking Opportunities

Some businesses I started came from others wanting my skills and wanting me to partner with them. A business client wanted me to build Virtual Office, a program to keep track of employees clocking in and out. An attorney wanted me to make Legal Checklist, a website that helped minimize the need for meetings and still brought the team together. A good salesperson with lots of passion for motocross wanted me to build Raceready to track racers and help them register online. Some business associates wanted me to help them with a company where we sold tax lien education and a tax lien book for investing. A friend wanted me to help him start Equity Innovators. I was helping out a companion and his son in Brazil, so I built olsbuild.com. I felt I was inspired to create lotocast.com, a music streaming service based on family values. Each of these businesses was very different from each other and came with their unique challenges.

But what if you don't have people asking you to make their applications or build them things? You have to start with your own idea.

When my wife and I were young, we needed quick money for rent. I went to a printing shop and asked if they had laser printer cartridges I could recycle. They gave me several empty ones they hadn't thrown away yet. I turned them into the recycling center and ended up with a lot more money than I thought, exactly what we needed! Why I didn't keep doing that and make a business out of it, I don't know. But there is a power in having a need and being willing to act on the opportunities that present themselves. Some of the best ideas come from needing a buck.

Building Confidence

Imagine hanging out at a party with your friends. It's fun and relaxed, and you're just yourself. Now, think about being at a party with big name people, billionaires, and your personal heroes. How do you feel about attending that party?

If you feel comfortable talking to anyone, like me, this is a blessing and will help you immensely in your business ventures. But you might feel a bit nervous or in awe if you are like most people. Conversations might feel stiff or cautious. You may be more careful about what you say, holding back your thoughts or opinions, if you get the courage to say anything to them at all. It's okay to be scared and intimidated. It happens to everyone at some point.

At a party with friends, talking should feel easy. You're open, laugh a lot, and everyone shares stories without pressure. Why is that? What makes you comfortable around them?

Put yourself in that scenario, at a party with famous or important folks. How do you feel? Is there this feeling that they're super successful and intimidating? Could you comfortably walk up to your hero in athletics, e-sports, science, or any other field and chat with them like a friend?

When I asked about what made you comfortable at a party with your friends, what did you answer? Perhaps because you and your friends share experiences or similar interests. Maybe you said it's because you feel they know you and you know they don't judge you. Deep down, everyone's just human. Even big-shot people have feelings, worries, and things they're unsure about. If you don't talk to someone, they will never get the chance to know you. When you chat with them, you see they're like everyone else. They have to put their pants on in the morning, just like you.

Let's go back to this hypothetical party. As you talk to the people who might be intimidating, you may realize that money or titles don't make someone more important than you. Everyone's experiences and feelings matter. It hits you that beneath the fancy stuff, we're all the same. Everyone brings something valuable to the table, no matter who they are. How does that affect the rest of your time at the party? What would you do if you saw these rich and famous people as equals?

You might not get an audience with anyone in the public eye right away; you may never meet your heroes in any particular field. In settings like the party I described, it's essential that you convey that you belong. You'd be surprised what results you can get by acting on the confidence you might not feel.

Ultimately, it's about understanding that no matter someone's status, they're still a person. Connecting with them on a fundamental level, sharing stories and experiences, that's what matters most. Everyone deserves respect and understanding, regardless of their fame or position. We're all equally important and deserve a chance to be heard and understood. So take that knowledge and act on it.

Mindset Change: Money Is Everywhere

I had a friend who started a rehab center for substance abuse. He began with one building and was able to pay for it outright. Once he proved he was making money, he reached out to investors with more of the attitude of "I'm letting you in on a good deal I've found" instead of "I need you to make my dreams come true."

The concept of money being accessible is an essential mental change. It helps if you have the numbers to back it, but if you believe in your idea and are willing to make it happen, you should act with that kind of confidence and excitement. In my town, a guy pitched the idea of building AC units for the moon. He raised enough money to get started on the project. The moral of that story is that there is money for people willing to go out and get it, regardless of the idea.

Knowledge will help you get far, but you will have nothing to show for what you have learned without applying that knowledge. In this light, I invite you to keep notes of your ideas while reading this book. The questions and exercises in this book have helped me when starting businesses and could help you solidify your ideas into opportunities. So, without further delay, what are you going to do? Do you need greater confidence in your vision? Or is it just an idea to begin with? If so, where will you put yourself this week to observe potential needs in communities or businesses? Who are you going to talk to that will help you realize we all are human when it all comes down to it? What would be the best way for you to see the world differently?

Kinds of Business

Many entrepreneurs, freelancers, contractors, and people who work for themselves must decide how much of their life they will dedicate to their business. Generally speaking, there are two kinds of businesses—lifestyle and occupational.

A lifestyle business is designed to sustain and support a particular lifestyle for the owner. It's usually centered around the owner's interests, passions, or hobbies. The primary goal is not necessarily to grow into a vast enterprise, but to maintain a certain level of income and flexibility that allows the owner to enjoy a specific lifestyle. These businesses often prioritize freedom, flexibility, and personal fulfillment over rapid growth or expansion. Most of the time, since the business revolves around you, if you stop working, it stops functioning. Some examples would be streamers, vloggers, singers, etc.

On the other hand, an occupational business is typically more growth-oriented and focuses on generating substantial revenue or market share. These businesses often require more time and commitment from the owner to scale and expand in competitive markets. The primary goal is to create a successful enterprise that may involve delegating tasks, hiring employees, and focusing on strategies for growth and profitability. These are the kinds of businesses you can sell, keep shares of, lease out, or hire someone to run on your behalf.

The critical difference lies in the primary objective of the business. A lifestyle business emphasizes maintaining a particular lifestyle while earning a living, whereas an occupational company aims for market growth and expansion. A question you will need to answer for yourself is: what kind of life do *you* want?

What's Your "Why"?

Why do you want to start a business? For some, it is because it pays better. For others, they enjoy the freedom to set their own hours. Some people are just done with having a boss and want to be in control of their own lives, while others still have a passion for some change they want to see in the world. For me, I wanted more time with my family. A lot went into it, as there usually is in life. But I wanted to choose who I worked for and to be there for my young family. Every time I worked for myself, it was a decision I made when I needed or wanted money.

Work like it is today was not always easy to get; you had to apply to many companies before you got an interview, and just because you got an interview did not mean you got the job. Growing up in the country, my only option was to work for the neighbors. There were not any jobs that I could apply for. In later positions, I could have easily gotten a high-paying job in the big city. But that sounded boring and starting my business idea sounded much more fun. (Not to mention the perks of my current job make it so I don't have to leave my house when it's cold outside, ha ha). I started working for companies as a programmer when I found an ad on Craigslist that a local company needed some temporary help. I answered the ad and have worked on the contract ever since. I am going on 20 years with this company because working for them fits my needs. If a job doesn't have a good work environment, doesn't pay enough for you to enjoy your life, or overworks you to a point where you struggle every day, go work for someone else! There are plenty of opportunities in this life. It might seem like a dream, but there is a way to make enough money and enjoy your life.

What Are You Passionate About?

I started a business in the last few years that I felt was very important. It was a music streaming service with 100% clean music and family values at its center. This venture caused me to put together a small company with employees and to learn a lot about advertising online. Nothing has come of this business at the current date, but it made me learn social media advertising, which helped me start my venture, Getsuccess101.

You might not always be able to start with your passion projects, but if you start a business doing something you already find boring, you will soon hate it.

What is something you don't mind doing for hours? What have you seen companies do that you would like to do? What challenges ignite your passion for innovation? What kind of life do you see yourself living?

When you think about businesses, do any resonate with your vision of positive change? Think about the things you have personal experience in and know. What have you learned that you struggled with learning? Think of a way to make learning more manageable for the next guy (that's why I'm writing this book). Maybe for you, it's a venture centered around mental wellness, offering support and resources for a healthier mind. Perhaps it's personalized learning platforms or mentorship initiatives designed to empower and inspire individuals to reach their full potential. Maybe you could teach people something you know that other people struggle with. I once knew a kid who scored high on his ACT in high school. Once he graduated, he began charging to be a personal tutor for high school kids preparing to take the ACT. He capitalized on what he knew and was able to make a difference in the process.

Being flexible is crucial in business. When you try different ways to make your company successful, it's essential to be open to changing your plans. Not every idea will work right away, and that's okay.

Learning from both successes and challenges is part of the process. Stay adaptable and adjust your strategies based on feedback and what's happening in the market. Being able to change and improve your business model shows resilience and a commitment to finding the best way for your company to succeed in a changing business world.

What Need Does Your Business Fill?

A successful business meets the needs of its customers. When a company provides products or services that solve problems or fulfills specific customer requirements, it gains their trust and loyalty. By focusing on what people truly want or need, a business attracts customers and becomes a valuable and vital part of the market. This ongoing process of understanding and meeting needs is essential for a company to thrive and stay relevant.

When I moved to where I live now, we found an old skating rink that wasn't being used above a gas station. My wife and I went up to the owner of the building and asked if we could use the rink. He said we could keep all the profit if we put in the work. He didn't even charge us rent! That job was enjoyable for me. In what other business do you have a room that people will pay you to just be in? It was a great deal!

Of course, we had to have the music, the lights, and coordinate the games, but that was all just fun. The reason it went so well is that in our city there weren't a lot of things for young people to do. Even though the location was far from town, the demand was so high that people would drive all the way out to us. If you see an opportunity, you should ask. You only know how it could turn out if you try it.

How to Choose an Idea

Pick Your Passion

If you are new at this and are just starting your first business, but you have a head full of ideas and need help figuring out where to start, I would pick one and run with it. Starting a business takes a lot of time and attention. If you have multiple ideas and lots of money, you can hire people to create your companies and then put more money into the ones doing well.

That takes a lot of capital, and if you are reading this, you probably aren't able to hire your ideas out.

Look to start your ideas by picking one, preferably the one you are most passionate about. One that you want, almost need, to go well. Here's why:

Once upon a time, you wanted to become a video game streamer. You like playing first-person shooters, but the popular game right now is raising a duck to win a triathlon. The playthrough is straightforward, and the streamers in this game are making bank. Should you stream this game?

You could. You might even make money. But even if you do, you will eventually get sick of the game and be stuck. Your fanbase for a game like that most likely wouldn't be the same as for the games you usually like to stream, so if you switched over to what you typically enjoy, you would probably lose most of your following.

For a real-life example, look at the author Sir Arthur Conan Doyle. He wrote essays, plays, poetry, historical novels, nonfiction works, and even works on psychic phenomena and the supernatural. What most will know him for is the beloved detective, Sherlock Holmes.

However, Sir Conan Doyle had a complex relationship with his famous creation. At times, he felt overshadowed by Holmes' popularity and wanted to focus on writing more "serious" projects. He even attempted to kill off Holmes, but eventually brought him back due to public demand.

In contrast, I was once a dance teacher for the dance style clogging. It wasn't the most money I have ever made, but I had a lot of fun doing it! I had taken over the class from a friend who wanted to retire. The class was about 130 students, and since then, I have had many classes of varied ages and sizes. I would still be teaching now if my knees kept up with it.

I took the job because I knew I would enjoy what I did every day. So, what could you do for hours and not want to pull your hair out? Which idea are you most passionate about?

Keep It Simple

Once you have the idea in hand, you need to create an exact plan for the bones of the business. This way, you can start with a basic model and know exactly what you are doing when you begin running it. Once you have the bare basics just right, you can eventually scale it according to the business profits and demand of consumers. By creating a simple version of your product or service, called a minimum viable product, you can test and improve without taking on too much at once. You don't want to start with your most complicated products or services. Whether you're working on apps, video games, electronics, or other services, this will keep your focus on progressing the fundamental parts of the business instead of trying to strengthen too many tendrils of your business that aren't vital.

For example, if you were to start a travel agency, you would want to start with the most straightforward and profitable thing to sell. Let's say, for this example, that you only sell cruises. It's a specific product with good returns. Mastering this first allows you to add more travel package deals or other destinations when ready. Once you've learned the ins and outs of selling cruises, you have most likely learned more about the legal side of things, the customer service, clients, financial risks, insurance, etc., that could have choked you if you had more things to balance. Doing this helps you learn the ropes without overwhelming yourself.

Once your base company is running smoothly, pay attention to what your customers say and make improvements. Learn from the process and slowly expand your business as you get more confident.

In summary, the idea here is to keep things simple initially. Starting small, learning, and then growing. Whether you're working on an app or a travel service, it is important to create something simple. Learn as you go, improve things, and grow your business when you're confident. This way, your entrepreneurial journey is not only manageable but also rewarding.

Scaling

Scaling refers to growing or expanding a business, typically to handle increased demand, reach a larger audience, or enhance overall efficiency. It involves increasing the capacity of a company to handle greater loads without compromising its performance or quality.

Scaling is a crucial aspect of business growth and sustainability, ensuring that as demand increases, a business can meet that demand effectively without sacrificing quality or customer satisfaction. It doesn't matter how much you scale if your customers leave bad reviews and you lose focus. Another thing is watching your profit margin. Make sure the company isn't getting bigger than what you can afford.

I have not done much scaling with many of my businesses. The life I like to live is usually well funded with the amount of work a small team or I can do. I have considered scaling some of my businesses, but I didn't need to become a powerhouse in any of my industries. You can be an entrepreneur without taking on larger projects than you want to; not every idea needs to be groundbreaking.

Different Markets

In the context of business and economics, a market refers to the overall environment where buyers and sellers engage in the exchange of goods, services, or resources. It's a space or a system that allows transactions to occur. Markets can exist in various forms, including physical locations like a traditional marketplace or virtual markets, such as online platforms. In a market, buyers express their demand for products or services, and sellers offer their goods or services to meet that demand. The interaction of supply and demand determines the price and quantity of goods exchanged in the market.

It's important to know what kind of market you are getting into. Markets can be categorized based on geographical location, product type, or consumer demographics. Understanding the dynamics of a market is crucial for businesses to make informed decisions and succeed in their operations. Here are some specific kinds of markets and how to tell them apart.

Saturated

Too many businesses out there

How to get into a saturated market is to *be unique.* Many people want to be songwriters, artists, novelists, etc. The trick is getting someone to buy *your* stuff compared to someone else's.

For example, people usually listen to music because they like the style or how it makes them feel. Ed Sheeran was good at combining his music with great videos. Pink Floyd was known for their biting political, social, and emotional commentary.

If you want to get into a saturated market, what makes your idea new and unique?

I ran a record company once. At the time, my family was performing a lot as a family show, the 5B's. We changed the show and the record company to the 7B's once my last two children were born. I mainly started the record company to produce my wife's music albums. I broke even in that venture, not making anything other than to cover costs. It didn't last long. In the artist world, be that performing or otherwise, the top 5% generally make money, and the rest have fun doing what they love.

Dominated

Corner on the market

These markets are hard to enter and hard to keep up. In the technology industry, everyone knows the Android/Apple battle. Imagine trying to be a third competitor in that fight for popularity. It can be done, but it would be challenging. The best way to succeed is by making their item or service better. In whatever market you are trying to enter, look at what you could do to improve upon the competition. Look very closely at the brand currently dominating the market and especially at the customers' reviews about what they like and dislike about the company. Look for the holes that people keep complaining about. If you can find a way to fix what the customers don't like, you will be the one they want to go to.

Be careful, however, as many people like advertising that "we are better than this other brand." In my opinion, that is just petty. Let your brand's marketing speak for itself. My company for tracking races was able to compete with the dominated market because we introduced the service of online registration in addition to monitoring the race. This service was something new that both the racers and the tracks wanted.

High Demand
Not enough to go around

High-demand markets are markets where everyone is clamoring for the service or product sold. Everyone needs a website. Everyone needs more medical staff. In markets like these, you only need to get yourself out there.

As a loan officer, I made a commission on the loans I would close. When the interest rate drops, people always look to refinance. I got into it right after a decline in the interest rate, so everyone I called said yes to my services.

If you want to get into a high-demand market, only take as many clients as you can handle. There's nothing worse than taking on too many clients and ruining your brand's reputation because you can't take care of them all properly.

The Golden Ticket

Every once in a while, you may "strike gold," if you will—Elon Musk, for example. Steve Jobs. People who had a dream and went for it, and the idea caught on. A lot of times, this is affected by circumstance and lots of luck. Hard work plays into it, too, but most people who find themselves in those situations wouldn't have dared to dream they'd be as big as they were when they started. I'll never say it can't happen, though.

How to Find Your Target Market

What Kind of People Are You Marketing To?

When I say "market," I often mean a specific demographic of consumers or the volume of businesses providing a product or service. The people who want your product or service are your "target market." Consider who would love what you're selling and who needs it. Once you know your target market well, talking to them and giving them precisely what they want is more manageable. Some primary things to consider when searching for your target market are:

- What kinds of people would use your product/service?
- What are the commonalities in those people?
- What is their age group?
- Where are they most of the time?
- How will your service or product benefit their lives?
- Could they afford the service or product? How will you get someone else to fund it for them if not?

As you pinpoint your target market, you will better understand how to reach them in marketing, cater to their needs, and provide a product or service that will entice them. When you know who wants and needs what you're offering, it's easier to speak their language and give them exactly what they want. Doing this helps you focus your efforts where they matter most, saving time and money. It also makes your business stand out because you offer exactly what your customers are asking for.

For example, consider a clothing brand like "Lululemon." They know their target market well: people who are into yoga, fitness, and leading an active lifestyle. Lululemon designs its clothes by focusing on comfort and performance. Their stores are often welcoming and offer community events like yoga classes. They understand their customers value style and functionality in their activewear. Using the above bullet points, what would the target audience of something like this be?

Taking this back to you and your ideas, what is *your* target audience? If it is ambiguous, try focusing on who would buy your service/product. Why are *you* offering it? If you want it, chances are someone else would, too, which brings us to the next part of the book.

How Many People Want Your Product?

Let's do a little exercise! Now that you know what demographic you want to market to, it's time to see if they are interested in your idea. I use this as a rule of thumb when looking into business ventures people bring to me or to see if my ideas will work.

First, find ten people in your target market you do not know (no friends or family, as they are sometimes biased).

The next step is to tell them briefly about your business. The key word is *briefly*. No one will want to stand there for five to ten minutes listening to a stranger talk about something that may or may not interest them. You should describe your idea as quickly and concisely as possible. Practice summing your idea up in three sentences. You can use more than that, but this exercise is to cut down to the bare minimum needed to explain your idea. When you ask people about your business, it doesn't have to be a whole pitch; it could be in everyday conversation.

Once you talk to someone about your idea, ask if it's something they would be interested in getting.

If ten say yes, that is high demand.

If five say yes, it's a good market.

If two say yes, you have an idea with little or no market, you will have to chip your way in or will want to find a new idea. I would only start a business if five or more out of ten said they would buy my product or service.

Networking

Making Friends

Networking involves building and maintaining relationships with individuals or businesses, often for mutual benefit. It creates connections, fosters relationships, and exchanges information or support within professional or social circles.

The primary purpose is to expand one's social or professional contacts, gain insights, share resources, and explore business opportunities through the network. The best way to network is to make friends with people. Not only will this help you not be lonely, but it will also enrich your life.

Whenever you need something, friends are there for you. In my mind, the whole purpose of going to college is to find good friends. A friend is someone you like, trust, and enjoy spending time with. They are there to support and share experiences with you. Real friends care about each other and stick together through good times and bad. It is important to put aside prejudice and see people for who they are. Being genuine in your interactions is equally important, regardless of who you are talking to.

People Just Like You

Find groups of people who like what you like. I network wherever I go and with whoever I associate with—when I'm at church, programming camps, with coworkers, clients, etc... I even network at a morning swim class I attend! Many of my contacts have come because of making friends in my workplace. Networking at college is excellent because you can get with those people anytime. Especially if you're getting the same degree, they will get hired at a company and can put in a good word for you.

As a computer programmer, I networked by going to code camp. I also networked by attending a local technical college luncheon with other business owners and influential people in my community once a month. Find relevant things going on in your community and show up to them.

I know I have said this before, but making friends is what you want to do. I can't emphasize this enough. You can get contacts and business cards, but having many friends will enrich your life and make things fun. Maybe you're thinking, "Friends are great, but if I market to them, they wouldn't want to hang out with me anymore." You're probably right. If you only collect contacts to market to them, that's being a salesman, not a friend. Friends should support your hopes and dreams like you support theirs. That doesn't mean they will all buy into your business, and it doesn't mean you should drop them as friends if they don't think your business will work.

Sales Groups

It is beneficial to network in places and groups of people that your target market frequents. It typically includes connecting with potential clients to exchange information, share insights, and explore business opportunities. The aim is to expand one's professional contacts, gain valuable knowledge, and generate leads or referrals for sales prospects. Networking in sales groups often involves attending events, participating in online forums, and engaging in activities facilitating relationship-building within the target community.

Resourcing

Go to where your competition is to see how they do things. Every month, my local college has an event where businesses pitch their ideas to investors. I am currently looking for some investors for a business that lacks funds but wants to hire me. I sent one of my employees to the event to network because I knew that was where our target market would be. He came back from the event with new contacts and will be setting up a meeting with one of them next week. We weren't part of the presentations, but by talking to people, we achieved our goal.

What does your business need? Where can you go? You can start by looking in your community and Facebook groups and at local events that may apply to whatever business you want to create.

Have Integrity

Friends help out friends. I had a friend who was highly placed in an advertising agency. He went through a hard time and lost his job. In addition to his career, he lost all his "friends." He was alone after that experience and realized all they wanted from him was what he could give them. They didn't want his friendship. You don't want to be a networker who has friends just to use them. Some people out there don't care. That can hurt, but don't let it poison you to become one. I have personally been blessed by having many of my employers and clients be personal friends in addition to being part of my daily business. I know you will be, too, if you let yourself be a friend.

My experience volunteering on a charter school board was because of a business client friend I had, who is now running for our state senate. I helped him out when he was in a pickle, so if I ever did call him up and needed something, we would have that natural connection pre-established. If you get contacts just to get contacts, you are a salesman and will be seen as such. People continually change and grow. Never underestimate the shy kid in the back of the class or any of your clients. Someday, they may be precisely the kind of person you need.

When you do a business deal in Brazil, you had better spend a day with the person before you pitch anything. If they don't know you, they don't trust you. If you bring too much business up before you get to know them, they will feel like you only care about the money. If you care about numbers and not people, you will live a lonely life as an entrepreneur.

If you only have a short interaction with someone and can leave them feeling better about themselves, not only did you help someone, but it will be easier to reach out to that person in the future. Especially if you already know they have a decently favorable impression of you.

Networking for Introverts

Networking can be intimidating, especially for introverts. However, mastering networking is essential for building professional relationships, advancing careers, and uncovering opportunities. Characteristics such as a preference for solitude, deep thinking, and sensitivity to stimulation can impact networking experiences, but they aren't impossible to overcome.

Many introverts experience anxiety when faced with networking, but there are strategies to help manage these feelings. Techniques such as deep breathing, visualization, and reframing negative thoughts can help introverts approach networking with a sense of calm and confidence. Most introverts have heard these techniques many times. My suggestions may not be new, but maybe they will give new insight:

Keep your end goal in mind. Why are you networking? Why is it important to you? Holding on to these things can motivate you to do what it takes to grow your networking circle.

Start out small. *Work with goals that stretch you but don't feel impossible.* Setting achievable objectives that push your limits but don't overwhelm you is key to making progress. By starting small and gradually increasing the difficulty of your goals, you can build momentum and confidence as you work towards achieving larger aspirations. Remember, progress is made one step at a time, and every small accomplishment brings you closer to success.

Establish regular conversations to have with people. *Have specific questions for conversations before meeting.* It's helpful to have some questions ready to start conversations or guide them where you were hoping they would go. Practicing self-introductions can help you feel more comfortable and confident when engaging with others.

Technology can be a valuable tool for introverts to connect with others before, during, and after networking events. Using social media platforms, professional networking sites, and email can help initiate and maintain relationships with industry contacts without the fear of face to face conversations.

Learning from Your Competition

I want to add a warning here about how it is good to learn from your competitors, but you shouldn't compare and get discouraged. While looking at your competitors, you might start feeling bad about what you have. You could begin to wonder why you are even trying since the other businesses you would be competing against look so good. This is an error in your thought process you will need to fix. If you think your company is trash, it will become trash. If you think, believe, and act like you are as successful as the businesses you are looking into, you will become that successful as you work for it.

Having competition is a good thing. It might seem counterproductive to have people selling the same thing as you, but it indicates that what you have will sell. It's like knowing you're playing a game people want to join. Competition tells you that there's a whole group of people out there who are interested in what you're doing. Imagine if you came up with a revolutionary and new product, let's say, a coin sorter. The product is a machine that you dump coins into, and it sorts them according to size. If no one else had anything like that on the market, you would have to teach people *why* they want it. They've lived this long without a coin sorter. Why do they need it now? But if you see a few coin sorters on the market and notice they are selling, you know your product will be bought as long as people can afford it. You should watch for their pricing, sales, and reviews in your competition.

Pricing

Keeping an eye on what your competition charges for their product or service will tell you how much people are willing to pay for what you will be providing. It helps you determine if your prices are fair or if you need to adjust them to attract more customers. Watching their prices can also give you ideas on offering better deals or making your products or services stand out. It's a way the economy keeps itself in check.

Sales

Understanding your competitor's sales gives you a good idea of how well the market is doing. By keeping track of their sales, you can see what's working for them and what might be popular with customers. It helps you learn from their successes and mistakes, giving clues on how to improve your business. It's an excellent way to learn from observation instead of your mistakes. Knowing their sales numbers can motivate you to aim higher and work smarter to win more customers. If what you want to market doesn't sell for other companies, you will want to look into why. Is their marketing slacking? Is it too expensive? Is there even a market for the product or service? These are some things to consider.

Reviews

Keeping an eye on your competitors' reviews is important when looking for potential needs, especially in a busy market. Those reviews tell you what customers like or don't like about your competition's products or services. By paying attention to reviews, you can learn from the strengths and weaknesses of your competitor's company. If customers love what they are doing, it might be worth considering for your own business. On the flip side, you can avoid making the same mistakes if customers are unhappy about something. It's like having a cheat sheet to make your business even better. This is why knockoffs generally burst into the market when a new market is started. If the customers aren't feeling heard, be there to support them, not blame the company they have been using. If customers complain about time or quality, ensure your product fixes those faults. You don't have to respond to every demand, but it's an excellent way to keep tabs on how your target market feels.

What If There Is No Competition?

If your product is either 100% original or you haven't seen it being sold or offered anywhere else, here are some possible reasons:

1. There is no market for it. Someone else may have tried, but it didn't catch on. People may not have wanted it at the time, which has happened to me a few times.
   Or
2. It's 100% original, and you will have to talk people into why they want it.

About ten years ago, before there was online shopping for grocery stores, I worked on a service to find the best price for groceries at nearby stores. The customers who would buy the app loved the idea. The stores, however, wouldn't give us the price information at that time. They wanted people to come into the stores so they could upsell them. Years later, you can price check online and even order it. I was ahead of my time, but that didn't mean it was a bad idea.

Branding

Choosing a Company Name

The best way to choose a name is to consider what you are selling or offering, and name your business according to that. For example, if you are selling rocks, "Rocks" is probably a good name that would make it easy to remember what you are called and what you do, especially if you have a memorable font (but more about that later). Keeping it simple and to the point is an easy way to be remembered. Of course, Apple makes new technology; everyone knows Apple because they made it big. It's the same with IBM computers or Purple mattresses. So, you can just call it something, and if you make it big enough, then people will remember you, but naming your company "Banana" for pet sitting may not be ideal unless you specialize in monkeys.

When looking into names for your company, make sure you are unique. Google what you are considering naming your company with quotation marks " " around the word so the search engine knows you want to search for that exact wording. Make sure to pick a short, easy-to-remember name. If I were a dentist and my last name was Smith, I wouldn't want to name my practice "Smith's" because if someone searched that name, they would get a grocery store, not my business. If you are into dentistry, health, medicine, etc., or some business where your service is the product you are selling, you may want to put your name in the title so people know who you are and can trust you. However, if you name a company after yourself, it makes it harder to sell someday. If you want to leave that possibility open, many medical, dental, massage, and other service-based companies will name their business after their location. For example, Dixie Eye Clinic or Red Rocks Rehab. They took the name of the community or something iconic in the city they were based in and used that in their name. The potential problem with that is if you want to expand your practice to other cities, "Red Rock" may seem strange in cities where that is not a common sight.

My point in that last paragraph is to remember what message you want to send with the name of your business. Is your company about what *you* can do for them? What about what your *service* is doing in the community? Maybe new tech you are working on? Carpets? Travel? Catering? Do you want to sell it someday? These are all things to consider.

Colors, Style, and Fonts

Just as important as your name is your logo and your style. Fonts can tell customers the difference between a bridal boutique and a place to pick up jeans. Based on colors and font, people will assume things about your brand. If you were to find a brand that had a swirly white font with light pink accents, but when you went to their website, it was blocky letters with dark blue, yellow, and orange, would you think you may have gone to the wrong place? Would you believe the business wasn't real? Maybe even think it was a scam?

Your business will need a "style guide" document with exact colors, fonts, and general vibes to have them all in one accessible place. This also gives you something to work off of when you get further into your marketing for advertisements and social media accounts.

Logos are an important way to identify your company without writing out who you are. Having something simple and straightforward is imperative. If you have too many details, when it is small, others may be unable to recognize it. Consistent colors, styles, and logos are significant for a company's success because they let people know who you are without saying a word.

As an example, let's look at Monster Energy Drinks. Monster's branding, sponsorships, and marketing strategies are geared towards a certain vibe. Their logo is plastered all over events like motocross, skateboarding competitions, and gaming tournaments. They sponsor athletes in these fields and create content that resonates with their target customers' thrill-seeking and energetic lifestyles. By aligning their brand so closely with these activities, they've become one of the first thoughts when people think of extreme sports brands. As such, they can market to people in that circle, and even all those wannabe people who don't want to feel bad about needing an energy drink to get through the day.

Your Brand's Voice

Brand voice is the prominent and distinct personality your brand takes on in all communications and serves to portray you in a certain way to your customers. As a defining characteristic of your marketing strategy, it allows you to connect with a specific audience that wants or needs what your company offers. As people who like volleyball will gravitate towards a volleyball court, people who like what you offer or sell will come to you if your brand welcomes them.

Let's take the brand "Apple" as an example. Apple has a distinct brand voice known for being sleek, innovative, and friendly. Their communication style is often simple yet sophisticated, focusing on creativity and thinking differently. When you read or hear Apple's marketing messages, they often use language that's easy to understand, with a touch of excitement about their products' capabilities. Their tone is conversational, but it also carries an air of expertise and reliability. Whether on their website, in their advertisements, or during product launches, Apple maintains a consistent brand voice that reflects their commitment to innovation and user-friendly technology.

On the opposite side of things, Wendy's, known for its fast-food restaurants, has a brand voice that's bold, witty, and sometimes a bit sassy. They're known for their playful and humorous tone, especially on social media. Wendy's engages with its audience by cracking jokes, cleverly roasting competitors, and using sarcasm in their interactions. Their brand voice is edgy and confident, often delivering quick-witted responses that stand out in the fast-food industry. Wendy's is fearless in taking a more daring and direct approach, setting them apart with their unique, entertaining, and, at times, aggressive brand voice.

Each of these companies has made its voice clear. People know what they are getting themselves into when they tag Wendy's. If Wendy's ever started "speaking" like Apple, or Apple like Wendy's, their communities would be confused, and they may even lose customers.

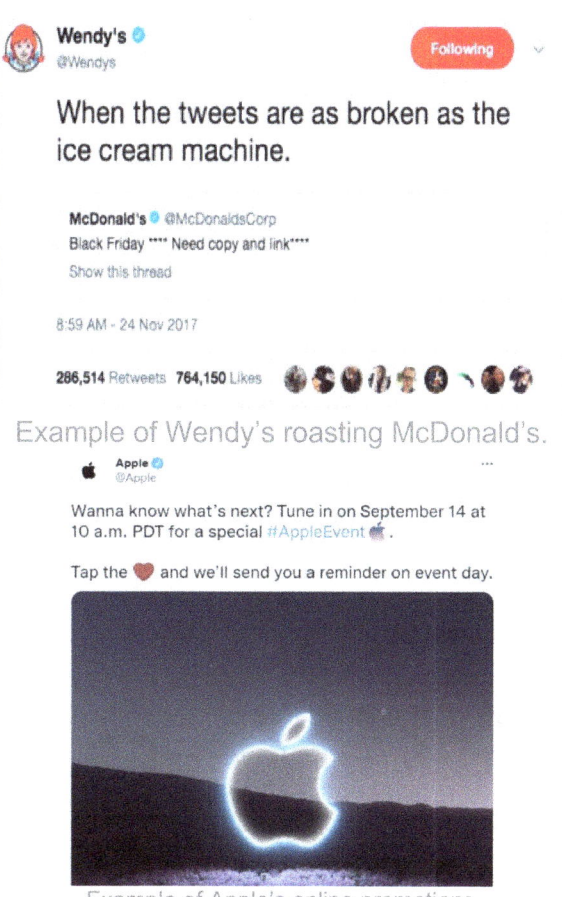

Example of Wendy's roasting McDonald's.

Example of Apple's online promotions

Marketing

Marketing is all about letting people know about products or services. In the online world, businesses use social media to connect with people. They also create valuable content to share with their audience, and they send emails with special messages to potential customers.

In the regular world, there are older ways of marketing, like putting ads in newspapers or magazines, showing commercials on TV or radio, and sending mail with ads to specific people. Some businesses also team up with famous people with many followers on social media to talk about their stuff.

Sometimes, businesses host or join events, conferences, or shows to display their products and talk to possible customers. There's also guerrilla marketing, where they do creative things in public spaces to get attention. When businesses want their ads to appear on search engines, they pay for that too.

There are lots of other ways businesses try to tell people about their stuff, like having other people talk about it, doing fun experiences, sending text messages, sharing content with other websites, asking customers to bring in new customers, making things go viral online, putting products in movies or shows, and more. How a business chooses depends on who they want to talk to, their industry, and what they want to achieve. They often use a mix of old and new ways to get the word out.

Social Media Tips

Social media marketing involves using platforms like Facebook, Instagram, Twitter, LinkedIn, and Pinterest to promote products or brands. The key to success is creating content, like posts, pictures, and videos, that appeals to your target audience, keeping your brand consistent across all platforms with the same logos, colors, and tone.

Engage with your audience by responding to comments and messages promptly. Use hashtags to increase the visibility of your content and consider paid advertising for more reach. Hashtags connect specific content and help the algorithm to know what to show and suggest to viewers.

Collaborating with influencers can boost your brand's visibility and engagement. Make sure it is consistent with your brand. If you sell basketballs and you get a makeup artist to advertise for you, they most likely won't do very well even if they agree to do it at all. Stay informed about platform algorithms and adapt your strategy accordingly. Different platforms respond to diverse kinds of posts. Analyze metrics to see how well your plan works and adjust it as needed. You can see analytics when you switch your social media accounts to business accounts.

Suppose you were to sell chocolate strawberries for Valentine's Day but also wanted to start a travel business. In that case, you may think beginning all your businesses on one social media account would work to gain followers for your business ventures. However, on social media it is more important that you are consistent with what you post and when than having a lot of followers. If you have 5,000 followers but only 30 likes on a post, that looks bad on the algorithm, and you will be shown to fewer people. You want to ensure your branding is consistent through your social media for each business venture separately.

In summary, successful social media marketing requires engaging content, staying consistent with your brand, interacting with your audience, and adapting to frequently changing trends and algorithms. This requires updating your personal knowledge almost constantly.

Turning Your Idea into an Opportunity

What Are You Selling?

One of the first things you should consider is something that may be obvious to some and rather difficult for others. What *exactly* is your business offering?

There are many kinds of businesses, but most can be simplified down to either selling a product or charging for a service. For example, Etsy sells crafts, while DoorDash charges you for the service of dropping off food.

A product business focuses on creating and selling tangible items. They manufacture or procure goods to sell to customers, like electronics, clothing, or books. Their main goal is to produce and sell physical things. On the other hand, a service business offers intangible assistance or work performed for customers. They provide services instead of physical products, such as consulting, education, or cleaning services. Their primary focus is on delivering specific expertise, support, or tasks to meet customers' needs without selling a physical item.

Deciding between a product-based or service-based business depends on what you enjoy doing, your skills, and what you want to offer to people. Consider what you're passionate about and what you're good at. If you're skilled in making or designing physical items, products may be for you. On the other hand, if you excel in providing advice, support, or performing tasks, a service-based business might suit you better. Think about what you want to offer to customers. Do you want to create something tangible that people can hold and use? Or do you prefer providing expertise, assistance, or solutions to people's problems?

Think about your target market. What are their needs or preferences? Are they looking for a specific product or a particular service?

Ultimately, the decision should align with your strengths, interests, and what you believe will resonate with your potential customers.

Most of my businesses, as of late, have been services. This is mainly because service businesses are great to start up due to their low or no upfront cost initially. Generally, your most significant cost in service businesses is your time.

For service businesses, you will want to get your full payment or half the amount upfront for expensive jobs. If not, you could get stiffed, and then all you can do is take them to court, which is rarely worth the price in legal fees. When making an agreement, it's better always to keep a "paper trail" or records of the deal, be that letters, emails, messages, or other proof you could show as evidence if needed.

How to Calculate Possible Costs

When I was a kid, I wanted to make money. I lived at the top of a hill; the nearest store was over six miles away. It generally took about an hour to ride my bike down the mountain, buy candy, and ride back. Google Maps will dispute me on the time it took. I looked it up once, and it said 44 minutes one way. Maybe I was just better at riding my bike back then, ha ha. I enjoyed the ride, too. Anyway, I would sell the candy on the weekends to neighborhood kids who lived in the area. I could have easily marked up the price two or three times what I was selling it for, but this was my first business, and I didn't know what marking up a product was then. Eventually, I got bored with selling candy at the table and paid my little brother to sell the candy for me. I stopped selling candy altogether because the product, time, and labor the business required were not able to support the business based on the price I was charging for the candy.

When deciding to start a business, it is important to know what resources you will need to start. Do you need a physical store location? A website? What will the manufacturing costs be? What about shipping or the costs of employees? There are many things to consider the cost of. I suggest taking a good amount of time to come up with a budget of how much you think your business will cost to start up and how much it will cost to maintain. Keep this budget, as you will need it later.

Something to keep in mind is when you buy products from a dealer, you are reliant on that dealer. I opened a phone store once called Helio, which depended on that one dealer. It was a month-to-month subscription for wireless services like T-Mobile. Soon after we opened, the company we bought phones from sold out to Virgin Wireless, a prepaid connection that left the value of our store competing with companies like Walmart, which wasn't worth it. So I was left with a bright blue building all setup and nothing to sell. At this point, you look at your options and move on, whether buying something else to sell or selling your contract on the building.

How to Markup Products and Why

Now that you know how much your business will cost, take the cost of your product or service (making sure to add into services how much the time you spent is worth), then add a margin to cover expenses and to make a profit. Here's a basic formula:

Selling Price = Cost Price + Markup

As an example, Abyte was my first company involved with computers. It was a computer IT service that went to smaller companies to help them switch over their files or reorganize them (this used to be harder to do than it is today). I charged high, 22 times the minimum wage at the time. I could have made my price more affordable if I wanted to be even more successful. But at this point in my life, I was looking for more money and fewer hours spent working; it worked for my needs well enough. Some companies still paid it, so I knew I could charge that much. In this example, one of my most considerable costs was my time. Make sure you account for that when pricing your product.

Photo of Brad Owen holding a cake to celebrate starting his business, Abyte.

To sum it up, first, you calculate the cost price. This includes all expenses related to producing or purchasing the product. It involves the cost of materials, labor, manufacturing, shipping, and any other direct expenses.

Next, decide on the markup percentage. This is the additional amount or percentage you'll add to the cost to cover overhead and generate profit. The markup percentage varies across industries and depends on factors like market demand, competition, and your business goals.

Determining a selling price is based on cost and markup. For example, if a product costs $50 and you want to apply a 50% markup to make it worth producing, it would leave the $50 product at $75 for anyone buying it.

Consider market research, customer perception, and competitor pricing when setting your markup. Finding the right balance between a competitive price and ensuring profitability is key.

Keep in mind your projected income and projected growth. If you're barely covering your costs, you won't have enough to expand, and you may want to consider if it is worth keeping your doors open. This depends on your point of starting a business, and that decision is ultimately up to you.

Marking Up for Your Time

Calculating the costs of your time is a fundamental aspect of understanding the value of your work and making informed decisions about pricing, productivity, and profitability. It's important that you charge a rate that accurately reflects both your desired income and the expenses associated with running your business or performing your work.

To begin, you'll need to determine your desired hourly rate – the rate at which you believe your time is worth based on factors such as your skills, experience, industry standards, and financial goals. This hourly rate serves as the foundation for calculating the costs of your time and represents the value you place on your expertise and labor. How much do you need to be paid to live your current life? How much would you like to be paid to live your ideal life?

As a general rule, I charge two times my costs for my product. If an employee who codes websites for me costs me $30 per hour, I will charge $60 per hour for programming the website. This is to cover my work of communicating with the company that ordered the website, making sure the website functions, any extra costs with my employee for bonuses and such, along with what I need to live my life and keep the company running.

Another way I decide the cost of my hours is based on my competition's prices. When it costs significantly less for me to produce a product than the current market rate, I bump my product price to what things are already selling for. For more about this, see the section "Learning from your competition".

This will have a few more steps for a business selling physical items but the principle is the same. For a physical business or product, you will need to estimate your annual expenses related to your business or work. These expenses may include overhead costs such as rent, utilities, insurance, equipment, software subscriptions, marketing expenses, and professional development. By calculating your annual expenses, you gain insight into the financial requirements of sustaining your business or work over the course of a year.

With your total working hours established, it's time to add your overhead costs into the equation. Divide your annual expenses by the total number of working hours to calculate your overhead cost per hour. This figure represents the portion of your hourly rate that covers your business expenses and is essential for understanding the true cost of your time. Make sure to take into account factors such as holidays, vacations, and sick days and provide a basis for understanding the total amount of time you have available for generating income.

After determining your overhead cost per hour, you can add it to your desired hourly rate to arrive at your total hourly cost. This total hourly cost represents the combined value of your desired income and the portion of your hourly rate that covers your business expenses. It serves as a benchmark for pricing your services and ensures that you're adequately compensated for both your time and the costs associated with running your business.

It's important to remember that not all hours worked are billable to clients or directly contribute to generating income. Non-billable hours spent on administrative tasks, marketing, client communication, and other business-related activities should be factored into your calculations to ensure that you're accounting for all aspects of your work.

Mission Statement

A strong vision sets the course for your business. A mission statement is a short and precise description of a company's purpose and what it aims to achieve. It outlines the fundamental reason for the company's existence, values, and primary goals. It's like the guiding star that directs the company's decisions and actions, reflecting its core beliefs and aspirations. A well-crafted mission statement communicates what the company stands for and its commitment to fulfilling its purpose in about a sentence. So, what do you want to capture in your mission statement?

Some examples of famous company mission statements:

Tesla: "Tesla's mission is to accelerate the world's transition to renewable energy."

Starbucks: "To inspire and nurture the human spirit—one person, one cup, and one neighborhood at a time."

Coca-Cola: "The Coca-Cola Company exists to benefit and refresh everyone who is touched by our business."

Estimated Profits

To project what your business might make in the future, start by understanding your market and customers. Estimate how much you could sell by looking at past sales, market trends, and your competitors' actions. This is how you will find your estimated revenue for a given period of time. Then, figure out all the costs of running your business. Product or service costs, paying employees, and other expenses are discussed in a previous section. After subtracting all those costs from your potential sales, calculate how much money you have left. Use this information to create a plan showing what your business expects to earn over time. Remember, it's just an educated guess based on your current knowledge. Things might change along the way, and that's ok if you adjust to the change. It is important to do so you know if your business will get off the ground.

Below is a basic formula for calculating estimated profits:

Estimated Profits = Estimated Revenue - Costs of Business

Investors, Rich Family, and Getting Money

What's a Pitch?

You may need extra funding if you have a bigger idea for a business that will take a lot more resources than you have to start up. You may need to pitch your business to an investor. You will need some data for your business to develop a compelling pitch of why someone should join you on a venture. It tells whoever you are pitching to some information about your business, why you believe it will succeed, and then data explaining what you will do with their money and what return they can expect from the company's growth. This data is essential to know about your business, even if you aren't going to pitch your idea or look for resources.

A pitch is a quick and convincing presentation where you try to sell an idea, product, or service. It's typically short and designed to grab attention and persuade others. It usually highlights the key points, benefits, and reasons why your audience should be interested or should invest in your offering. Pitches are often concise, impactful, and tailored to your target audience. But before writing a pitch, you need to know what you are pitching.

Working with Partners

There are pros and cons to working with partners. You can learn from each other, utilize each other's networks, and have someone to share fresh ideas and perspectives with. However, people are complicated and can make business confusing when ideas don't combine nicely. Some advantages of partnerships are:

Different Skill Sets: Partners have different skills and perspectives, making the business more rounded. Many partners who have approached me had an idea and needed a programmer with my skill set. I can do programming, and they can pitch the idea to businesses. Complementing and diverse interests make for good partnerships.

Shared Work: Partners share jobs, so no one has too much to do. One partner handles ordering products and shipping, while the other takes care of talking to customers, running the employees, and managing the face of the business. This can help with not getting burned out by learning and being responsible for too many things simultaneously.

Money Help: Partners can give money to help start or grow the business. Partners can put their own money in or get loans together with a combined credit score. Partners also often expand your networking circles, which can help you find investors.

Sharing Problems: If something goes wrong, partners work together to fix it. For example, If one partner is sick, the other can cover for them. You also have two minds working on any given problem in the business. Two minds can be better than one.

Making Friends: Partners know different people, which can help the business. Networking with two people can be more effective than one, especially if the partners are in different social circles.

Having a partner means you also have to share the revenue with someone. You must figure out how to split it to keep the business running. There is also the factor that, as people, we are prone to miscommunication, which can lead to hurt feelings, defensiveness, and mistrust. Some disadvantages you may face:

Different Ideas: Partners might have differing views on what to do, causing problems. For example, if one partner wants to sell one way, and another wants another, or you need to decide what product to sell, this can cause contention and a pause in production and profits.

Sharing Money: Partners have to share the money the business makes. If the business earns $100,000, partners have to split it. At which point is it 50/50? What if one partner did all the selling, all the advertising, all the work, and the other partner was the one who had the original idea but wasn't really involved? Is it still fair to split 50/50?

Waiting for Decisions: Partners need to agree on decisions, which can take a long time. Making quick changes is hard because everyone has to say "yes."

Personal Money Risk: Depending on the partnership, partners might have to pay for problems with their own money. Partners might have to pay from their pockets if the business owes money. Whenever it comes to finances between people, things can get dicey.

Leaving is Hard: If a partner wants to leave, it can be difficult and cause problems. If one partner wants to stop working together, sell the business, or branch off and start their own business that may end up being competition to the one you created together. It might be hard to figure out what's fair.

Balancing Workload: Sometimes, one partner feels they have done most of the work and deserves more pay. Both partners may feel they put more into the business than the other. This can cause a lot of conflict, especially if you have different ideas of where the company should go or if one partner wants to sell the business.

Flakey Commitments: When relying on a partner, you have to trust them to do their part. If either partner doesn't prove reliable, this could cost the business money and time. In my experience, this has been the most common experience with partners. Partners may say they will do things and then lose motivation. What if you lose motivation while in a partnership?

Closing the Idea: What will you do if the business is struggling and turns out more work than you deem valuable? If you don't feel the venture is worth it for you anymore but you have a partner, that could lead to contention, whereas if you want to try something different without a partner, it's easier to change course.

Before starting a business with someone, talking, understanding each other, and writing down what everyone agrees on is essential. Make sure you think through potential touchy areas such as percentages of profit, financial responsibilities, or ownership. That way, you can come to an agreement *before* you have other pressures and responsibilities.

An example of a business where I was a minor partner was a coaching business, teaching people how to buy tax liens. The salespeople made some good sales in the first month, and our business looked like it would be successful. Those I was working with decided they did not want to put the money back into the company. Instead of using the money to buy more leads, they decided we should all keep our cut and pull out, so we had to close the business. No leads meant no one to call and no more income. It would have been a good business if those I was working with decided to keep going.

The best business partners I have had were when we were not legally connected as partners but contracted as two businesses that worked together. A good example of this kind of partnership was an installation company I was a part of. I installed wireless cell phone signal boosters in large companies like Boeing and Microsoft. It took two weeks for clearance to get into Microsoft's server building. The place was huge! I got to ride a lift, probably 150 feet up in the air, installing an indoor antenna. While I lived in Seattle, this guy approached me and said, "I need an installer. I would rather do the sales than the installation. If I do the sales, would you do the installation?" I asked how much he was going to pay. His offer was 2.5x a day what I was making at my job in the city, and that same rate applied to anyone I needed on my team. I had no idea how to install these kinds of cables, but for that price, I knew I could learn! We did not share revenue or anything in each other's business, so there was never any argument over percentages. Responsibilities were clear, and both fulfilled our ends of the deal.

A partnership worked well in my lawn mowing and snow shoveling business. We split everything based on who did the work instead of 50/50. Again, I technically would have owned the company, and my friend helped complete the job. I made the sales, and he helped fill the service end of it. We were partners in workload, although if there had been paperwork, it would have been solely my business. The only risk you have in this kind of a partner is if they don't do their side of things. I made an online program with a partner split 50/50. She didn't do her part of our business, so now I'm left with a product I haven't done anything with.

When you start a company, make sure you keep at least 51% of the ownership. This way, you stay in charge and make the big decisions. Try not to give away too much of the company to others. By keeping most of the ownership, you get to keep most of the company's money, but more importantly, you have the final say when the decisions are made.

If you partner with family, ensure expectations are communicated clearly and agreed upon. Working with family is different for everyone since every family is different. Many who work with family suggest writing out expectations and making a contract to avoid one side or the other feeling overworked or used. I have worked with my children on many ventures. I had a performing group with my wife and our children. Since then, I have worked with them in many kinds of businesses, and I still have some work for my companies. My wife always says we make more money when our children work for us.

 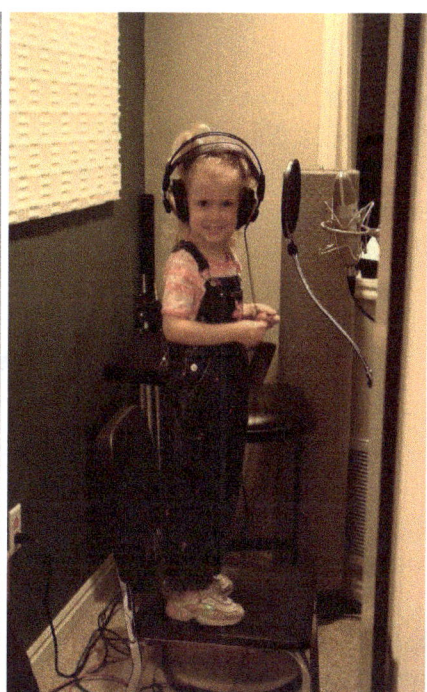

The Owen Family at the OC Tanner.
The youngest Owen girl in a recording studio.

My brother-in-law and I also started a food stand as my children grew up. The original idea with that business was to open a dinner theater serving the best steak you've ever had. My brother-in-law had the idea, but I was unsure about partnering with him on a high-cost investment. We spent two weeks perfecting the recipe for a hamburger seasoning as a test. During that time, both of our families ate a lot of hamburgers! Once our recipe was down, we bought a tent and a spot selling gourmet hamburgers at local fairs and festivals. It went well, and we had a lot of customers! After about a year, it became apparent that we wouldn't be able to do a long-term business due to my brother-in-law not fulfilling his end of the bargain we had agreed on.

Family and Friends

Starting a business is risky. To avoid disaster, never risk things that would cause disaster. Something vital to learn early on is never to risk someone's living or house for your idea. High-risk ventures should never be funded with money that is needed for survival—be that yours or anyone else's.

There *are* people out there with money, lots of money. On Facebook, you are only three contacts away from somebody else worldwide! If you don't personally know anyone with lots of money, networking is the name of the game. Start with something like this to people you know: "Do you know anyone who would be interested in investing in _____?" You'll be surprised at the results you can get by asking around.

My son bought a business filling vending machines. When the idea was introduced, he didn't have money to buy it outright, so he had to raise it. However, his wife had a brother who had a lot of money, so he pitched his idea and was able to use that money to buy the vending machines. This brother had enough money that he would not miss it if it never got paid back.

Angel Investors vs Opportunity Investors

The thing to know about investors is they want to make their money multiply. If you can do that, you will have a happy investor. The kind of investor you are looking for at the beginning of a business is an "angel investor."

An angel investor is an individual who provides financial backing for startups or early-stage businesses, usually in exchange for ownership equity in the company. Angel investors are often seasoned entrepreneurs, successful business professionals, or high-net-worth individuals looking to invest their funds into promising ventures. Their investments can range from a few thousand to several million dollars. Angel investors typically play a hands-on role in the businesses they invest in, offering mentorship, advice, and networking opportunities along with their financial support.

On the other hand, an opportunity investor seeks investment opportunities across a broader spectrum. They focus on various investment opportunities that might yield substantial returns. This type of investor isn't necessarily confined to early-stage businesses or startups. They might be interested in diverse investment vehicles such as stocks, real estate, commodities, or companies across different stages of development. Unlike angel investors, who may be more involved in the growth and development of the businesses they invest in, opportunity investors are often more focused on the potential returns and scalability of the investment.

Angel investors specifically target early-stage or startup companies, providing financial support, mentorship, and expertise. Opportunity investors cast a wider net, exploring diverse investment opportunities primarily focusing on potential returns, often across various stages of a business or different asset classes.

You can expect to pay back investors 10x-30x what they give you eventually. You can lose this money, and it's no harm, no foul. They won't miss the money. They expect two out of ten ideas to work. It's up to them to know the risks and make that decision. It's your job to give them the option to multiply their money through your idea.

No two businesses are the same, and neither are any two types of investors. Carefully research every kind of investor, noting who's looking for what and what they're offering in return for their funding.

No matter what type of investor you seek, a business plan and accurate financial records are crucial to help take your company into the next phase.

Other Options for Money

Stockholders

When people buy stock in a company, they mainly want two things: to make money and to have a say. They hope the value of their shares goes up over time and that they get a piece of the company's profits in the form of dividends. They also want to know what's happening in the company and have a say in big decisions, like having a voice in how things are run. They're looking to make money and be part of what's happening in the company they've invested in.

Foundations

Foundations want to team up with companies that care about similar things. They look for businesses that share their values, like caring for the environment or helping people. Companies willing to work together on projects that positively impact society or the environment catch their eye. They also prefer companies that are open about their work and show how they use their resources responsibly. Basically, foundations seek partnerships with businesses that want to make a difference in ways that match their own goals.

Grants

Grants give businesses free money they don't have to pay back. This money helps them research, grow their business, or start new projects without using their own funds. Getting a grant also makes a business look good and trustworthy. It can bring new opportunities for working with other companies and getting special training. Some grants also support businesses doing good things for their community or society. Grants offer money and perks that help companies to grow and do more. Grants.gov is a website you can search for available grants and apply for them.

Partnering with a College

Partnering with a college to start a business can be helpful. You get access to intelligent people like professors and students who can give you advice and new ideas. Colleges often have money and programs to help start businesses, and they can introduce you to other important people. Plus, being linked with a college makes your business look more trustworthy. You can also find great students from the college who might want to work for you, bringing fresh energy and ideas to your business. Overall, teaming up with a college gives you lots of support, connections, and potential employees that can make your business stronger.

Bootstrapping It

Bootstrapping a business means starting and growing it using your resources, personal savings, or revenue generated by the business itself instead of relying on external funding from investors or loans. It's about being self-reliant and using whatever you have at hand to get the business off the ground. This is the way of starting a business I am most familiar with.

This approach often involves keeping costs low, being frugal, and finding creative ways to fund and grow the business without taking on outside debt or giving away ownership to investors. Bootstrapping requires a lot of hustle, resourcefulness, and careful financial management to sustain and grow the business using limited resources.

Bootstrapping a business offers the advantage of full autonomy and financial independence. You retain complete control over decisions without relying on outside investors, avoiding debt and the pressure for immediate returns. This approach fosters resourcefulness and creative problem-solving, encouraging innovative solutions to challenges. However, resources might be limited, making it hard to grow. The slower growth trajectory and personal financial risk are also factors to consider. Despite these challenges, bootstrapping allows for 100% ownership of the company and a steady, self-reliant approach to business growth.

Raising Money

You need to ask for money if you don't have it on hand. Asking for money in business can be as easy as asking your rich uncle or professional investors.

I once had a friend working on the Great Salt Lake for a brine shrimp company. He thought he wanted to start his own brine shrimp harvesting company and decided he would need a new fishing boat and some other things, including some licenses. The license cost was very expensive and was renewed yearly. The boat was a significant investment, and the total he needed was around the price of buying three medium-sized houses outright. He had a rich uncle, so the uncle gave him the money and invested it in his company. He was partners with his father, and the investor (his uncle) said he would only invest if they took out a life insurance policy on both him and his father. His father passed away many years later, so the uncle was able to collect the initial investment. It's brilliant if you ask me.

You will likely need documents about your business to continue growing your idea. Paperwork can be confusing and complicated, but don't let it discourage you. Google is an excellent resource for terms you don't understand, as is an AI to put words into easier-to-understand explanations. In the following few sections, there will be a decent amount of step-by-step and paragraphs on the purposes of this paperwork. Not every company will need all this. But most businesses and business owners should be familiar with them.

To start, what do you need to know to officially pitch your company to get the money you need to start? That depends on the kind of business you create and how much money you need. If you go to official investors instead of a wealthy family member, you may need documents like:

Executive Summary

What need is your company filling? Why would the investor invest in you? What's your plan? The executive summary is a quick rundown like a cover letter to get an investor to listen to you. In this document, you will cover the problem and say what you are going to do to fix the problem and how much it will cost. In other words, why do you need money, and how will you use it?

Pitch Deck

Once the Investor is willing to listen to you, you'll want to show them a PowerPoint or a file of pages telling them about the company and how you will spend their money should you receive it. A pitch deck is typically concise and to the point, aiming to grab the investor's attention and convey critical information effectively. While there's no absolute rule, a standard pitch deck usually consists of 10 to 20 slides. Each slide in a pitch deck should focus on a specific aspect of the business, such as the problem being solved, the solution offered, the market opportunity, the business model, competition, financial projections, the team, and the ask (funding or support needed). The goal is to deliver a compelling and comprehensive business overview within a relatively short presentation, usually around 10-15 minutes, leaving room for questions and discussion.

Prospectus

A prospectus is a formal document, the legal side of things, that provides details and information about an investment offering to potential investors. It's usually issued by companies or financial institutions when they plan to sell stocks, bonds, or other securities to the public or investors. The prospectus includes essential information about the investment opportunity, such as the company's financial health, operations, the risks involved, how the funds will be used, and other relevant details. It's designed to help investors make informed decisions by providing a comprehensive overview of the investment opportunity and its potential risks and returns. The prospectus is regulated by financial authorities to ensure transparency and accuracy of the information supplied to potential investors.

Writing a prospectus involves several key steps:

Company Information: Begin with an overview of your company, including its history, mission, and objectives. Describe the industry, market trends, and your position within it.

Details of the Offering: Clearly outline what you're offering—whether it's stocks, bonds, or securities. Specify the amount offered, the price, and how the funds will be used.

Financial Information: Provide financial statements, such as balance sheets, income statements, and cash flow statements. Include details about revenue, expenses, profits, and losses.

Risk Factors: Identify and explain potential risks associated with the investment. Discuss market risks, competition, regulatory risks, and any other factors that might affect the investment.

Management Team: Introduce key members of your management team, including their expertise, qualifications, and contributions to the company.

Legal and Regulatory Disclosures: Include legal information, regulatory compliance, and any pending litigation or regulatory issues that might impact the investment.

Executive Summary: Summarize the key points of the prospectus concisely and compellingly. This section should give potential investors a clear understanding of the opportunity.

Remember, a prospectus needs to be accurate, clear, and compliant with regulatory standards. It often involves collaboration between legal, financial, and marketing teams to ensure all necessary information is included and presented effectively. When preparing a prospectus, seeking professional guidance or consulting legal experts familiar with securities regulations is recommended. This might be intimidating, but investors are worth it.

Private Placement Memorandum

A private placement memorandum, PPM, is for your "seed money" prepared for your investors to start the business. It is a legal document used in private securities offerings to provide detailed information to potential investors.

Here is an example PPM for a fictional tech company:

> Private Placement Memorandum
>
> Fictional Tech Innovations, Inc.
>
> Executive Summary:
> Fictional Tech Innovations, Inc. offers a private placement of its common stock to accredited investors. This document outlines the company's background, current financial status, and the purpose of the offering.
>
> Company Overview:
> - Brief history and mission of Fictional Tech Innovations, Inc.
> - Description of products or services offered.
> - Overview of the management team.
>
> Terms of the Offering:
> - Total offering amount and number of shares offered.
> - Price per share.
> - Minimum investment amount.
> - Use of proceeds.

Risk Factors:
- Discussion of potential risks associated with the investment.
- Market and industry-specific risks.
- Regulatory and operational risks.

Financial Information:
- Historical financial statements.
- Projections for the future.
- Use of funds.

Management:
- Bios and qualifications of key executives.
- Compensation structure.

Legal Information:
- Securities law compliance.
- Terms and conditions of the investment.
- Investor rights.

Subscription Agreement:
- Details on how investors can subscribe to the offering.
- Subscription terms and conditions.

If your company needs more money, your idea is big, and you are talking in the millions, you may need to pitch to people with more money. Remember, people are just people, and there is money for those with a passion and an idea.

IPO and Private Funding

An IPO, or Initial Public Offering, is when a company invites everyone to become part-owners by selling its stocks for the first time on a stock exchange, like a grand opening to the public. This allows the company to raise a lot of money from many investors.

Companies that are ready for an IPO are often in a mature stage. They've grown enough, proved they can make profits, and want to expand even more. It's like saying, "Hey, we're doing well, and we want more people to invest in our success." An IPO is like a company's big moment, stepping into the public spotlight and sharing its success with the world.

Regulation A (Reg A)

Regulation A is like a fundraising party for smaller companies. Instead of going the traditional route and inviting a few big investors, these companies want to include everyone—regular folks like you and me. It's a way for these smaller companies to say, "Hey, we're doing something cool, and we want you to be a part of it."

Companies at different stages can use Regulation A, but it's often chosen by businesses that aren't quite ready for a full-blown IPO (Initial Public Offering). These companies might be growing and need some extra cash to expand their ideas. Regulation A allows them to ask many people to chip in some money and be part of their journey. It's like a smaller, friendlier version of going public.

If you're thinking about using Regulation A (Reg A) for your business, you need to check a few things. First, Reg A has two tiers. Tier one lets you raise up to a certain capital annually. Tier two lets you go up to a higher capital. Both tiers let regular people and wealthier investors join in. Check online for specifics on numbers and how it would benefit your business.

To get started, you have to file something called an offering statement with the SEC, explaining what your business is about and the details of your offer. If you go for Tier two, you'll also need audited financial statements. Once you're up and running, you'll have to keep reporting to the SEC regularly. You don't need to worry about how much money your investors make or have; it's open to everyone. However, you do have to share a lot of information about your business, including financial statements.

Regulation Crowdfunding (Reg CF)

Regulation CF is like a fundraising get-together for small companies that want support from their community. Instead of asking big investors for a lot of money, they can ask regular people—friends, family, or anyone interested—to pitch in. It's like saying, "We have this cool project, and we'd love your help to make it happen."

Most of the time, these small companies turn to crowdfunding sources to spread the word. They use online platforms to reach a broader audience. So, Regulation CF is not just about raising funds; it's also about connecting with a crowd of supporters who believe in the company's vision. It gives an opportunity to spread the word. Instead of just getting a product, you become a part-owner of the company.

Check a few important things to determine if you can use Regulation Crowdfunding (Reg CF). Your business has to follow specific rules to qualify. Reg CF lets small businesses get money from the public using crowdfunding platforms. First, it should be set up under U.S. laws and not be too big. There's a limit to how much money you can raise. Check online to see the limit for your kind of business. You'll need to work with registered crowdfunding platforms that connect your business with potential investors. You'll also have to share important details about your business and how much money you're looking for. To keep things fair, there are rules about how much money each person can give based on their income and net worth. If your business fits these rules, you might be able to use Reg CF.

To begin the Regulation Crowdfunding (Reg CF) process, you'll want to contact a registered crowdfunding platform. These platforms act as intermediaries, connecting small businesses with potential investors. Examples of crowdfunding platforms include StartEngine, SeedInvest, and Wefunder. You can visit their websites and usually find information on how to get started. They guide you through the steps, helping you understand the requirements and assisting with the necessary documentation. Remember that working with a registered platform is a key part of using Reg CF, ensuring compliance with the rules set by the Securities and Exchange Commission (SEC).

Regulation D (Reg D)

Regulation D is like a special club for companies that want to sell their stocks to a select group of people, usually sophisticated investors or institutions. It's a way for these companies to say, "Hey, we're doing something exciting, and we want specific folks who understand our business to join in."

Companies at different stages can use Regulation D, but it's often chosen by more established businesses that are not quite ready for a public offering. These companies might be in a growth stage, already making profits, and looking for a bit more cash to expand. So, Regulation D is like a VIP pass for them to invite certain investors to join their journey without going through all the public fuss. It's a quieter way for companies to share their success with a chosen group.

Starting a Regulation D (Reg D) offering involves several steps. To make sure you are doing it right, you will want to hire a business attorney to do it for you.

Taking on a Business Partner

Business partners are like teammates in a game. When people decide to start a business together, they become partners. It's like saying, "Hey, we're good at different things, so let's work together to make something awesome."

Business partners share the responsibilities and rewards of the business. They might have different skills—one could be great at talking to customers, and the other might be excellent at numbers. Together, they help each other succeed.

These partnerships can happen at any stage of a business—from the very beginning, when the idea is just starting, to later, when the company is growing. It's like having a buddy to share the journey, make decisions together, and celebrate successes as a team. So, business partners are like co-captains steering the ship of their business adventure.

Licensing

Business licenses are an essential legal step for regulating businesses at different levels, such as local, state, and federal. They ensure legal operation industry compliance and uphold safety, health, and ethics standards. Licenses are linked to tax obligations, aiding in tax tracking and collection. They contribute to consumer protection by signifying adherence to standards and quality assurance. Additionally, licenses play a role in zoning, supporting record-keeping, and generating revenue for governments. Check with local authorities for specific requirements, as they can vary by city, county, and state. Industries like massage, hair, and food have unique licensing needs and need to stay informed about changes as regulations evolve.

Getting business licenses involves identifying relevant permits, understanding regulations, contacting local authorities, and gathering necessary documents. Completing license applications, submitting required paperwork, paying fees, and undergoing inspections if needed. It's crucial to be diligent in meeting licensing obligations for overall business success and legal standing.

This all sounds pretty scary, but in the business arena, they will tell you if you make a mistake. One thing you don't do is ignore the IRS. You call them up and work with them. If you get a fee from the IRS and you don't know about whatever it is you did wrong or didn't do, you could ask if they can waive it as you fix what the problem was. Make sure you don't do it twice, though. Once is an accident and a warning; twice is seen as intentional.

For example, I started a real estate investment business with my friend. It worked like this: We would get people to buy stock in the company, and we would buy real estate with that money. The investor would share in the appreciation value of the business.

After submitting a legal document to the State Department, I got called into the state office, and they told me if my company took money from people's homes or mortgages, then both my partner and I would go to jail. My business partner had previously lost other people's money in an investment business that came from second mortgages. If I had known that before, it would have been a huge tip for me not to go into a business venture with him. They continued saying that if he was caught doing it again in our new business, we would both go to jail and be charged with fraud since my partner had already been warned. Obviously, after talking to my partner, we stopped.

City License

A city license is often called a business or municipal license. It covers various aspects of a business's operation within a specific city. The exact coverage can vary depending on local regulations, but a city license typically includes legal authorization for the company to operate within the city limits. It ensures that the business complies with local laws and regulations.

City licenses often address zoning regulations, ensuring that the business operates in a designated zone approved for its type of activity. This helps maintain a balance between residential and commercial areas. They are also often linked to local taxes. They help the city track and collect various taxes, such as sales or local business taxes, contributing to municipal revenue. The license serves as a record of the business's existence and activities within the city. It allows local authorities to maintain an accurate database of companies in their jurisdiction.

City licenses protect consumers by ensuring businesses follow specific standards and regulations. This can include ethical business practices and fair treatment of customers. In some cases, revenue generated from city licenses may be used to fund public services and infrastructure improvements within the city. For businesses that involve public health and safety concerns, such as restaurants or healthcare facilities, the city license may include compliance with health and safety standards.

Overall, a city license is a comprehensive tool that covers legal, regulatory, and financial aspects to ensure businesses operate responsibly within a specific municipality. Specific coverage details can vary, so companies need to understand and comply with the requirements set by their local government. If you are unsure if you need a city license, you can always go to your city office and ask.

County License

A county license grants legal authorization for a business to operate within the broader geographical area of a county, covering both unincorporated regions and potentially multiple municipalities within that county. It ensures that the business complies with county-level regulations, including zoning rules and specific standards applicable to areas outside city limits. The county license may be associated with county-specific taxes, contributing to the county's revenue for services and infrastructure. Essentially, it is a comprehensive permit allowing businesses to conduct operations lawfully within the county's jurisdiction, aligning with local regulations and facilitating responsible business practices. Again, ask your county office if you need one, and they will tell you.

State License

A state license is a crucial legal requirement for businesses operating within a specific state's jurisdiction. It grants official authorization for the business to conduct operations, ensuring compliance with state-level regulations and standards. A state license is often mandatory in starting and running a business, regardless of size or industry. The license may cover various aspects, including zoning rules, health and safety regulations, and industry-specific requirements mandated by the state government. Additionally, state licenses may be linked to taxation, with businesses contributing to the state's revenue through various taxes, such as sales or business taxes. A state license is a foundational element of regulatory compliance, providing businesses with the legal authority to operate within the designated state boundaries.

A state license is typically required when operating a business within a specific state's jurisdiction. The need for a state license arises from the state's regulatory requirements and is often a mandatory step for legal compliance. Here are common situations when you may need a state license:

1. Starting a Business: When establishing a new business entity within a state, you will likely need a state license to operate legally. This applies to various business structures, including sole proprietorships, partnerships, LLCs, and corporations.

2. Changing Business Activities: If your business changes its activities, expands its services, or enters new industries, you may need to obtain additional or modified state licenses to align with the updated scope of operations.

3. Relocating the Business: Moving your business to a different state requires obtaining a state license in the new jurisdiction. Each state has its own set of regulations, and compliance is essential for legal operation.

4. Industry-Specific Regulations: Certain industries, such as healthcare, finance, or transportation, have specific licensing requirements at the state level. Businesses in these sectors must secure the relevant state licenses to meet industry standards.

5. Selling Goods or Services: You'll likely need a state license if your business sells goods or services within a state. This

ensures that your business complies with state laws and regulations related to commerce.

6. Professional Licensing: Individuals in professions like law, medicine, real estate, or accounting may require professional licenses issued by the state licensing boards to practice legally.

Researching and understanding the state's specific licensing requirements where your business operates is important. Contacting the state's licensing authorities or regulatory agencies can provide detailed information tailored to your business type and activities. Regularly reviewing your compliance status and updating licenses as needed ensures that your business operates within the legal framework set by the state.

Home Occupation License

I should just say this for most licenses. When in doubt, ask your city. A home occupational license, often called a home-based business license, is a permit issued by local authorities that allows individuals to conduct business activities from their residence. This license type is crucial for running a home-based business while ensuring compliance with local regulations. Obtaining a home occupational license typically involves an application process where individuals describe their business activities and address any potential impact on the neighborhood. This permit is especially relevant for small businesses and entrepreneurs in consulting, freelance work, or online services. It provides legal authorization for conducting business activities within the residential setting, allowing individuals to balance professional pursuits with the convenience of working from home. Home occupational licenses contribute to the formalization of home-based businesses and help maintain harmony between residential and commercial interests within a community.

Specialty Licenses

Specialty licenses refer to specific permits or certifications required for businesses operating in specialized fields or industries. These licenses go beyond general business licenses and are tailored to certain professions' unique requirements and regulations. Examples of specialty licenses include professional licenses, such as those for doctors, lawyers, accountants, and architects, which require specialized licenses to practice. These licenses ensure that individuals have the necessary education, training, and expertise in their respective fields.

Businesses in the health and wellness industry, such as fitness trainers, massage therapists, and nutritionists, often need specialty licenses to operate. These licenses may involve demonstrating specific qualifications and adhering to health and safety standards. Certain trades, such as electricians, plumbers, and contractors, may require specialty licenses. These licenses typically involve meeting specific skill and competency requirements to ensure the safety and quality of services.

Businesses selling and distributing alcoholic beverages, such as bars, restaurants, and liquor stores, often need special licenses to comply with state and local regulations. Entertainment and event industry businesses, such as concert venues, theaters, and event planners, may require specialized licenses to operate legally and ensure public safety.

Businesses in specialized fields need to understand and obtain the necessary specialty licenses to operate legally and meet industry standards. These licenses often involve specific qualifications, inspections, and adherence to regulations unique to the nature of the business.

Legally a Business

Sole Proprietor

A sole proprietorship is a simple way to run a business. In this setup, one person owns and runs the whole thing. The owner has complete control over decisions and daily tasks. Unlike fancier business structures, starting a sole proprietorship is more manageable, with fewer rules to follow. This makes it a good choice for small businesses, freelancers, and people who want things to be simple. But there's a big thing to consider: the owner is personally responsible for any business's financial problems. This means their own stuff could be used to pay business debts. On the bright side, all the money the business makes goes to the owner, and they report everything on their personal tax forms, making taxes more straightforward.

Shoveling snow under your own name, like I did when I was a youth, would be an example of an unofficial sole proprietorship. Once you hire someone or create a business name, you need a license because people don't know who you are, and the government doesn't know who to tax.

DBA

When you decide to conduct business using a name other than your legal name, you must register a "Doing Business As" (DBA) or fictitious business name. This registration is for ensuring transparency and compliance with local regulations. Typically, the DBA process involves filing the necessary paperwork with the appropriate government agency, often at the county or state level, depending on your location. This registration is essential for sole proprietors, partnerships, or corporations that choose to operate under a name that doesn't match their official business name.

To register a DBA, fill out the necessary forms with details about your business and the alternate name. This helps authorities track businesses in their jurisdiction. Once approved, you gain the legal right to use the name, though it doesn't grant exclusive rights.
If your company is big enough to consider forming a corporation, I recommend having an accountant for taxes and consulting with them. The right choice depends on business goals, ownership structure, and taxation preferences. Different forms of corporations suit specific needs and preferences in the business world.

C Corporation (C Corp)

A C Corporation (C Corp) is a standard corporate structure that separates the business from its owners (shareholders). One big advantage is that it protects shareholders' personal assets from business debts. C Corps can have lots of shareholders and sell different kinds of stock. Shareholders don't run the day-to-day operations; they pick a board of directors who choose officers to handle business affairs.

C Corps can last a long time, even if ownership changes, which is good for businesses with big, long-term plans. But there's a challenge—C Corps might get taxed twice. First, the company's profits get taxed, and then if those profits are given to shareholders as dividends, they might get taxed again on their personal income tax.

While the C Corp offers advantages, they have more rules and paperwork. Businesses should think carefully about their long-term goals and how much they're willing to deal with the additional requirements.

S Corporation (S Corp)

An S Corporation (S Corp) is a tax-friendly choice that lets income pass through to shareholders without facing corporate taxation. This means the business itself doesn't get taxed on its profits. Instead, shareholders report their share of the business's income on their personal tax returns. It's a way to avoid the double taxation that can happen with C Corps.

However, there are some rules for S Corps. They can only have a few shareholders, and all shareholders must be U.S. residents or citizens. Also, S Corps can only have one class of stock, limiting the types of shares they can issue.

Choosing an S Corp is a good move for small to medium-sized businesses looking to save on taxes. Following the rules and ensuring the S Corp structure aligns with the business's goals and shareholder requirements is essential.

Limited Liability Partnership (LLP)

Due to its distinct advantages, a Limited Liability Partnership (LLP) is preferred among professionals like lawyers and accountants. One protection it affords partners is ensuring that each partner is shielded from other partners' business-related actions or debts. This protection extends to personal assets, minimizing individual risk.

An LLP offers flexibility in management, allowing partners to tailor the internal structure to their preferences. This adaptability is especially helpful in service-oriented industries where collaboration and shared decision-making are common. Pass-through taxation is another feature of LLPs, allowing profits and losses to flow through to individual partners and preventing the double taxation often faced by corporations.

Establishing an LLP involves registration with state authorities and following state-specific regulations. A comprehensive partnership agreement is crucial, outlining each partner's rights, responsibilities, and expectations. Professionals within an LLP often secure professional indemnity insurance to mitigate risks associated with professional negligence claims.

While an LLP provides a blend of liability protection and management flexibility, it requires compliance with state regulations, careful drafting of partnership agreements, and adherence to dissolution processes if needed. Overall, an LLP is an effective structure for collaborative service industries, offering legal protection, tax benefits, and adaptability in management structures.

Limited Liability Company (LLC)

A Limited Liability Company (LLC) is a versatile business structure combining corporate and partnership elements. One of its key advantages is providing limited liability protection to its members (owners), safeguarding their personal assets from business-related liabilities. This means that members are not personally responsible for the company's debts or legal actions, offering a layer of financial security.

LLCs offer flexibility in management and taxation, allowing members to choose how they want the business to be taxed. They can opt for pass-through taxation, like a sole proprietorship or partnership, where the business's profits and losses flow to the individual members' tax returns. Alternatively, an LLC can choose to be taxed as a corporation, benefiting from specific corporate tax structures.

A distinctive feature of an LLC is its ability to shield individual members from the actions of other members, similar to a limited liability partnership (LLP). This means that if one member engages in wrongful or illegal conduct, the other members are generally protected from personal liability.

While an LLC provides many advantages, it's crucial to note that proper legal and financial practices are essential for its successful operation. Members should have a clear operating agreement that outlines the rights, responsibilities, and profit-sharing arrangements among members. This document helps prevent misunderstandings and disputes down the line. Additionally, maintaining a clear separation between personal and business finances is important for preserving the limited liability protection offered by the LLC structure.

Choosing the right business structure is a critical decision, and an LLC's flexibility, limited liability, and taxation options make it a popular choice for many small businesses and startups.

Nonprofit Corporation

A friend of mine in Utah found an old movie theater and decided it needed to be fixed up and repurposed. He put together a board and got them to fundraise for the project. He had the project as a nonprofit and had the nonprofit hire him as executive director. True, he could be fired from his own project in this way, but it would be nonsensical because he has the passion and the vision for the project. He was getting paid by his own idea because he got someone else to fundraise for him. This is a great example of when there's a will, there's a way to get the funding.

Nonprofit corporations are dedicated to serving charitable, educational, or community-focused purposes rather than making profits for shareholders. These organizations aim to benefit the public and must adhere to specific regulations to maintain their tax-exempt status. Nonprofits often have boards responsible for making crucial decisions, and regular meetings are required to discuss and vote on various matters.

A president or a similar executive role typically oversees the day-to-day operations. It's important to note that while nonprofit corporations can't distribute profits to individuals, they can still generate revenue, which is used to further their mission.

Understanding the unique structure and regulations governing nonprofits is crucial for those involved in these organizations. Regular board meetings, adherence to tax-exempt guidelines, and effective leadership are key elements in the successful operation of nonprofit corporations. Engaging with professionals specializing in nonprofit management can provide valuable guidance and support in navigating this structure's specific requirements and challenges.

B Corporation (Benefit Corporation)

B Corporations, or B Corps, are businesses that focus on making profits and social and environmental goals. These companies commit to meeting high standards and impacting society and the environment while staying transparent and accountable.

To become a certified B Corp, a company has to thoroughly evaluate its practices, looking at how they affect people, the environment and how it's governed. This process ensures that B Corps are living up to certain values that go beyond just making profits. Being transparent is crucial, as B Corps have to share information about how they operate, their impact, and how well they meet the established standards.

Choosing to be a B Corp is a big decision for businesses that want to be socially responsible. It shows a commitment not only to financial success but also to caring for people and the planet. Nowadays, consumers, investors, and employees appreciate and support companies that prioritize social and environmental responsibility, making B Corp certification a meaningful recognition for those wanting to impact the world positively.

Close Corporation

Close corporations, also called closely held corporations, are characterized by having a restricted number of shareholders, often consisting of family members or a small group of investors. Unlike larger corporations, close corporations follow a more relaxed structure with fewer formalities. This structure allows for a more personalized and intimate approach to business operations.

In a close corporation, the shareholders typically have close relationships or shared interests, creating a more tight-knit business environment. This limited number of shareholders promotes a sense of familiarity and often leads to a more agile decision-making process. Additionally, close corporations often benefit from reduced regulatory requirements and less stringent reporting obligations than larger corporate entities.

While the close corporation structure offers flexibility and simplicity, shareholders need to define their roles, responsibilities, and expectations clearly. Establishing a well-drafted shareholder agreement becomes crucial to navigating potential conflicts and outlining the corporation's operation rules.

Understanding the dynamics of a smaller, closely held group of shareholders is vital for those considering a close corporation. It provides an alternative to larger corporations' more formal and complex structures, offering a balance between personal relationships and efficient business management.

Business Insurance

Embarking on the business journey comes with inherent challenges and risks, making business insurance a useful investment. Business insurance comprises various components, each serving a specific purpose in fortifying a business against potential threats. Property insurance shields assets from unforeseen events like fires or thefts, while liability insurance offers legal protection in the face of claims regarding the business's responsibility for injuries or accidents.

Business interruption insurance covers financial losses during pauses in business operations. Workers' compensation supports employees in case of work-related injuries and is required in some states.

Commercial auto insurance assists in accidents or damages involving business vehicles. Cyber insurance defends against online threats.

The ability to customize insurance coverage is crucial, allowing businesses to tailor protection to their unique needs. Ultimately, business insurance is a financial safety net, offering stability and ensuring businesses can navigate unexpected challenges without succumbing to severe financial hardships. Understanding and selecting the right insurance is a strategic move for businesses, ensuring resilience in the face of unforeseen challenges.

Hiring an Accountant

Staying informed about tax rules and deadlines is essential, and professional help ensures the smooth handling of tax complexities associated with having employees. Accountants assist with quarterly and yearly taxes, potentially saving you money. While you might think you can't afford an accountant, having employees may make it more feasible. The savings in taxes that accountants provide can offset the cost, contributing to the overall financial health of your business. I started using a professional accountant when my accountant friend told me if I could afford employees, I could afford someone to do my taxes. He was right because the accountant saves you money in taxes in the long run. It's their job to keep up to date with the best ways to handle taxes.

Schedule C

A Schedule C is a tax form used by sole proprietors, freelancers, and single-member LLCs to report their business income and expenses to the Internal Revenue Service (IRS). It is attached to the individual's personal income tax return (Form 1040) and helps calculate the net profit or loss from the business.

On Schedule C, you list your business income, deduct eligible business expenses, and arrive at your net profit or loss. This figure is then transferred to your personal tax return, contributing to determining your overall taxable income.

It's crucial for individuals operating a business as a sole proprietorship or single-member LLC to accurately complete Schedule C to comply with tax regulations and ensure they are reporting their business income and deductions correctly.

PNL

A Profit and Loss Statement (PNL) is a financial tool for businesses. It helps you understand if your business is making a profit or facing losses over a specific time. You can use it to make informed decisions, manage expenses, and set financial goals. The PNL is also essential for communicating with investors, lenders, and stakeholders, providing a clear picture of your business's financial health. It supports tax compliance, aids in creating budgets, and allows you to compare your performance against industry standards. Ultimately, a well-prepared PNL is vital for effective financial management, planning, and decision-making in your business.

To write a Profit and Loss Statement (PNL), you would need to:

1. Gather Financial Data: Collect details about your revenue, cost of goods sold (COGS), and operating expenses.

2. Revenue: List all sources of income, including sales, services, and any other revenue streams.

3. Cost of Goods Sold (COGS): Identify and calculate direct costs of producing goods or services.

4. Gross Profit: Subtract COGS from the total revenue to get the gross profit.

5. Operating Expenses: Sum up all operating costs, such as rent, utilities, salaries, and other overhead.

6. Operating Income: Deduct operating expenses from gross profit to obtain the operating income.

7. Other Income and Expenses: Include any non-operating gains or losses.

8. Net Income Before Tax: Combine operating income with other income and subtract other expenses.

9. Income Tax: Calculate taxes owed on the net income.

10. Net Income: Subtract income tax from net income before tax to determine the final profit or loss.

Ensure accuracy in your figures, categorize expenses properly, and use clear language. PNLs are vital for assessing a business's financial health and making informed decisions, usually within a fiscal quarter or year.

What Is a Fiscal Quarter?

A fiscal quarter, often referred to simply as a quarter, is a three-month period used for financial reporting. Companies commonly divide their financial year into four quarters spanning three months. These quarters are labeled Q1 (January, February, March), Q2 (April, May, June), Q3 (July, August, September), and Q4 (October, November, December). The specific months may vary depending on the company's fiscal calendar. Using fiscal quarters helps businesses and investors track financial performance and make comparisons over regular intervals.

Knowing fiscal quarters is important for businesses and investors as it provides a structured way to track and analyze financial performance. Companies use fiscal quarters to report their financial results regularly. Investors and stakeholders rely on these reports to assess a company's health, growth, and profitability over time. Breaking the financial year into quarters allows for a more granular company performance analysis. It helps identify trends, seasonal variations, and areas needing attention.

Businesses often set goals and strategies based on quarterly performance. Understanding how the company is doing each quarter helps adjust plans, allocate resources, and make informed decisions. Investors and analysts often discuss a company's results in the context of fiscal quarters. Being aware of the quarterly performance helps in effective communication with stakeholders. In addition, the financial markets are accustomed to companies reporting results quarterly. Meeting, exceeding, or falling short of market expectations each quarter can impact a company's stock price and overall market perception.

Knowing fiscal quarters is important for effective financial management, strategic planning, and communication within the business and with external stakeholders. It provides a regular rhythm for assessing and responding to the dynamic nature of the business environment.

Balance Sheet

A Balance Sheet is a financial statement that provides a snapshot of a business's financial position at a specific moment. It presents the company's assets, liabilities, and equity, giving an overview of what the business owns, owes, and its net worth. The balance sheet follows the accounting equation: Assets = Liabilities + Equity. It is a crucial tool for assessing a business's financial health and stability. Investors, creditors, and management use it to make informed decisions and understand the company's overall financial standing.

I've only ever used one to give to my accountant, but they are used to assess a company's financial health by presenting its assets, liabilities, and equity. It helps stakeholders understand the business's resources, obligations, and overall net worth at a specific point in time. Investors, creditors, and management use the balance sheet to make informed decisions about the company's financial stability and performance.

While a PNL shows the net income or loss over a period, a Balance Sheet highlights the company's financial standing at the end of that period. They complement each other, providing a comprehensive view of a business's financial performance and position.

1099 Contractor

A 1099 contractor, or independent contractor, is an individual or business offering services to another entity without being considered an employee. The "1099" refers to the tax form used to report the contractor's income, distinguishing them from employees. Independent contractors manage their own taxes, including Social Security and Medicare contributions. Businesses hiring 1099 contractors don't withhold taxes or provide typical employee benefits. While this arrangement offers flexibility, contractors bear specific tax responsibilities. The 1099 series encompasses crucial tax forms for reporting various incomes to the IRS. The 1099-MISC, for example, reports miscellaneous income like payments to contractors. Other variations cover interest, dividends, securities sales, and pension distributions. Receiving a 1099 signals income beyond regular wages, requiring accurate reporting for tax compliance.

EIN Federal Tax ID

An Employer Identification Number (EIN) is a federal tax identification number issued by the Internal Revenue Service (IRS) to identify a business entity for tax purposes. Also known as a Federal Tax Identification Number (FTIN), the EIN is used by businesses, trusts, estates, and various entities when filing tax returns, opening bank accounts, applying for business licenses, and handling other financial transactions.

The EIN is a unique nine-digit number, similar to a Social Security Number, but designated for business entities. It helps the IRS track and identify businesses for tax reporting and compliance purposes. Businesses typically need an EIN if they have employees, operate as a corporation or partnership, or engage in certain financial transactions that require this identification.

Applying for an EIN is a straightforward process and can be done online through the IRS website (irs.gov) or by mail, fax, or phone. It's essential to fulfilling federal tax obligations for businesses in the United States.

You need to obtain an Employer Identification Number (EIN) for your business in several situations. Firstly, the EIN is essential for tax withholding, reporting, and payment purposes if you plan to hire employees. Additionally, if your business operates as a corporation or partnership, regardless of employee count, having an EIN is a requirement. When opening a business bank account, most banks will request an EIN to facilitate the separation of personal and business finances. Filing federal tax returns for income, employment, or excise taxes also necessitates using an EIN.

When applying for business credit or loans, lenders often require your business to have an EIN. Some states may also mandate an EIN for state tax purposes, and if your business operates a Keogh Plan or falls under specific trust, estate, or nonprofit categories, obtaining an EIN is necessary. It's crucial to note that obtaining an EIN is a free process and can be done through the IRS website or by mail. Ensure that your business activities align with the need for an EIN to comply with tax regulations.

Employees

Understanding payroll details becomes important as your business grows and you hire employees. Handling taxes when you have employees involves deducting federal income tax, Social Security tax, and Medicare tax from their pay based on their Form W-4. You also need to contribute your share for Social Security and Medicare, matching what you deducted from employees. Additionally, you must pay federal and state unemployment taxes to support unemployment programs.

Proper reporting involves forms like the significant Form W-2 detailing your employees' earnings and taxes deducted. Depending on your business location, state and local taxes may add complexity. Hiring a professional accountant or a business specializing in this area can simplify the process.

Hiring People

This is a different subject, but I am adding it because I do interviews differently than most. With any hiring, you want to build a team in your business. Loyalty comes with being treated right and having clear expectations that can be fulfilled; it is not something you can buy.

For most large corporations, you fill out an online application that automatically screens the applicant. If the applicant passes the automatic screening, then the applicant either takes another test or gets a group interview or a personal interview, followed by one or two interviews until the applicant gets offered the job.

Since I am one person and I decide who gets the job, I look at the resume to see if they, at the minimum, list the skill I am looking for as a skill on their resume. I look at their history of where they used the skill and then find out how many years they have used that skill in a working environment. I then ask for a portfolio demonstrating the skill. After that, I schedule an interview. If they pass the interview process and I am still confident they can do the job and will work for the amount I have budgeted for that job, I give them an assignment. This assignment is usually very simple and should take them less than an hour to accomplish. If they accomplish the task without being paid, without me having me follow up with them, and within the time frame that was agreed upon, I mark their name in green on a spreadsheet, indicating that they would be a good fit for the job. If they do not finish the assignment or follow up with me (I don't follow up with them on purpose), they won't work in my work environment and will receive a rejection letter.

Then, I review the list and offer the job to the one who requires the least pay. Usually, I only have to offer one or two people the job, and then they accept.

Extras

I've been through the ups and downs of starting many businesses, and there are many ways to go about it. I share my experiences here, hoping they might be useful to you on your entrepreneurial adventure. Starting a business is different for everyone, but maybe my stories can give you some tips and encouragement. Your journey will have its unique twists, but sharing them is worth it if my experiences can help make your path smoother. I wish you creativity, resilience, and success in your business endeavors! This last chapter will be about my experiences with things that aren't necessarily starting your own business, along with warnings, pitfalls, and possible distractions I've seen hinder new entrepreneurs. I hope it helps.

Arrogance

Jumping into a business idea without market research is like setting sail without checking the weather. Thinking your idea is good is essential to an entrepreneur, but assuming it's a hit without understanding what your potential customers want or need is a risky gamble. Market research is like your compass, guiding you through the seas of consumer demand. Without it, you might be in rough waters, facing low demand, fierce competition, or a market that doesn't resonate with your idea. Taking the time to explore your market before diving in ensures you navigate confidently, adjusting your sails to align with the currents of genuine opportunity.

When to Hire People

If you don't know how to do something, you can either learn or hire someone to do it. People are amazing and can learn nearly infinite things, but with time and interest, it's not always ideal for you, as a business owner, to do everything. Let's say you figure out how to open a store for exercise clothing, and it pops off! You work all day, every day, and your business is thriving! You may want a life back to enjoy the hobbies you haven't had time for since putting your all into this business. You may want to hire someone to do a job you don't like or one that would give you more time if someone else could learn how to do it.

The salvage store we opened in Seattle was around 3,000 square feet, which was quite large. We were open six days a week from 10:00 am to 8:00 pm. It would have been a long day if you were to do it by yourself; the problem is we just couldn't do it ourselves. When a truckload of goods was received, we needed to unload the 60ft truck in an hour or less. We did not have a dock or a forklift, and we unloaded the truck by hand. I could not do it all myself. The entire family helped, but we needed more help, so we had to hire people. The store had two cash registers. I could not manage them both, so we had to hire another person to help with the cash register. We stocked the store shelves as we unloaded the truck. I also needed help because people are messy. They make a mess of your store, take things off your shelf, play with them, and then leave them on the ground, blocking the aisle. We had at least two people at the store at all times just to keep it running.

Processing Failure

Failure means different things to different people, as does success. In business, it often means not reaching your goals or facing challenges that prevent your business from succeeding. It can include losing money, struggling in the market, or stopping your business.

Navigating setbacks requires a thoughtful approach. First and foremost, it's essential to acknowledge and process the emotions that accompany failure. Frustration, anger, disappointment, sadness, and anxiety are all natural reactions to setbacks and failed attempts. Allowing yourself to feel these emotions is a crucial step in moving forward. However, there is a difference between allowing yourself to feel and getting stuck in your feelings.

I had a real estate website-building company called Kiosa. I made a basic website that was partially customizable. I worked with real estate agents, and they wanted way more features than I was prepared for. It took too much time, and I wasn't covering how much time it was costing me. Some could say that business "failed." If I had stayed in any of my "failed" businesses, I could have made them work, but it came down to "Do I really want to keep doing it?" When I get bored with an idea, I tend to move on, which is how I can confidently say I have never failed.

If you started a business and got millions of dollars in debt and they took your house, business, car, and all your money, I could maybe call that a failure, but I have never faced such a tragedy. If you aren't careless, you should be able to avoid such calamities. Failed attempts, mistakes, and bad business investments **aren't failures**.

"The only real mistake is the one from which we learn nothing."- Henry Ford.

That is the only real failure, too. Failure is only a failure when you go into the depths of despair or have learned nothing from it. Then you have truly failed. The only absolute failure is staying stuck in it. Choosing to stop there is the only time it is permanent. Success is enjoying what you are doing, whether you make money or not, at least in my mind.

Zeosha is a company that has a YouTube channel we worked on full-time for two years. We spent thousands of dollars on good equipment and thousands more on professional editors. We have not been monetized yet, and we have spent a lot of money. However, the thing about a video platform like YouTube that we learned is that viewers don't care about how high-quality things are; they care about the content.

People intentionally make things low-quality for comedic purposes. Most shorts seemed to be filmed from a cell phone, we are still doing it today even though the company has not made any money. I don't see Zeosha as a failure but as a learning experience and something I enjoy doing. I have never failed. I've never let myself see things as failures.

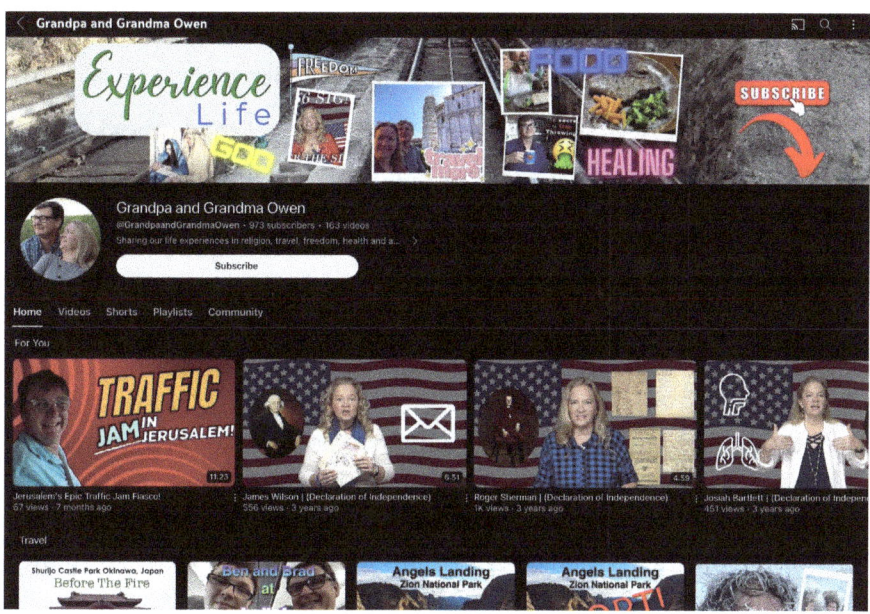

If you feel you have failed, treat failure as a valuable learning opportunity, extracting lessons that can inform and improve future endeavors. Seeking feedback from mentors, peers, or customers can provide valuable insights into areas of improvement and offer diverse perspectives on the situation. Remember your why, and don't let the setback or anyone's feedback discourage you from trying again.

Setting realistic expectations is important, understanding that not every venture will succeed immediately. Remember that setbacks are an inherent part of the entrepreneurial journey, and they do not define your capabilities. Many successful entrepreneurs have faced mishaps before ultimately achieving their goals.

Celebrate small wins, acknowledging and appreciating progress, no matter how minor. Building resilience is a continual process, and maintaining a long-term perspective is crucial. Use setbacks as a source of motivation to refine your approach and persistently work towards your goals. In summary, mistakes or setbacks are not the end. Failure is a choice. Anything can be a learning experience to gain valuable insights and personal development.

MLMs and Pyramid Schemes

I have joined around 35 MLMs over my lifetime, I think, most when I was younger. I know how to make good money in an MLM, but I am unwilling to do the work. Most startup MLM companies don't last more than a few years. You put in a lot of work to make good money, and then the company goes out of business.

When I was working at a successful company selling a food supplement product, we looked at going with an MLM distribution method, but the markup on the product would need to be seven times. The normal markup is two times, which would make the product unaffordable. If you choose to head in this direction, ensure you are "on top," if you will. The higher you are in the MLM, the better money you will make.

While Multi-Level Marketing (MLM) and pyramid schemes share certain similarities, they are distinct.

In an MLM, participants earn commissions from their sales and the sales of the individuals they recruit into the business. MLMs often involve legitimate products or services and focus on product sales. The structure forms a tiered network of multiple levels.

On the other hand, a pyramid scheme is an illegal and fraudulent business model. In a pyramid scheme, the emphasis is primarily on recruiting new participants, and the money flows upward through recruitment rather than selling products or services. Pyramid schemes are unsustainable and often collapse, leaving those at the bottom with financial losses.

While MLMs have a legal framework and can be legitimate businesses, evaluating each opportunity carefully is essential. Some MLMs may exhibit characteristics that raise concerns, and it's crucial for individuals to thoroughly research and understand the specific structure and practices of any MLM they consider joining.

Scams and Dead Ends

Detecting whether an opportunity is a scam involves researching and considering several red flags. Even after a thorough investigation, you can still be caught unaware. Here are some indicators that can help you identify potential scams:

Too Good to Be True. If an opportunity promises unrealistic returns, especially with minimal effort or investment, it's likely a scam. High rewards with little risk are often a warning sign. If you feel it could be a real opportunity, go to my next tip.

Check Reviews and References. Research the opportunity online and look for reviews or testimonials, specifically for reviews not attached directly to their website or an affiliate link. A lack of positive feedback or numerous negative reviews is a warning sign. If you can't find anything on the internet about them, that could be a signal, too.

No Clear Business Model. Scams often lack a transparent business model. If it's unclear how the opportunity generates revenue or sustains itself, you may want to ask more serious questions.

Lack of Transparency. Legitimate opportunities provide clear information about the product, service, or investment. If details are vague, and the promoters avoid answering questions, it's a red flag.

Payment for Training. If someone is looking to hire you and asks for money for training or hiring fees, they are more than likely just offering hyped-up training for a certain price. Often, this will switch you into an independent salesperson for them, and you will have to pay to be a part of that.

Request for Personal Information or Money. Scammers may ask for personal information, upfront fees, or payments through unconventional methods such as gift cards. Legitimate opportunities usually don't require payment in advance or sensitive personal information right away.

Pressure Tactics. Scams often use high-pressure tactics to create a sense of urgency. Be wary of opportunities that push you to make quick decisions without proper consideration.

Unprofessional Communication. Poor grammar, spelling mistakes, and unprofessional-looking websites can indicate a scam. Legitimate businesses maintain a professional image.

Trust Your Instincts. If something feels off or too good to be true, take the time to thoroughly investigate before committing to any opportunity.

Always conduct due diligence, research thoroughly, and seek advice from trusted sources before engaging in any opportunity, especially if it involves significant financial decisions. Once, I helped in the legitimate business of real estate trusts. This type of business works as follows:

Imagine someone has a property and is paying 4% interest for their mortgage. Mortgage interest is now at 6%. You want this property but don't want to pay the current mortgage rate. There is a way to keep the mortgage at the original rate, and that is to assume the mortgage. If you partner with the original owner and have them keep 10% of the interest in the property, you pay them, and they pay the mortgage. You form a trust and share in the appreciation.

An attorney approached me and asked me to build an automated system to create the contract automatically for real estate trusts. They used it for partnerships between people who didn't have good credit scores and those who had good scores and could buy a house at a lower interest rate. I just created the software. Thinking back on this experience, I realize it could be easily set up as a fraudulent business, so be careful before investing in things.

Door-to-Door Sales

Door-to-door sales have benefits like establishing a personal connection and immediate feedback for adjusting the pitch. It allows for a targeted approach to specific areas or demographics. However, drawbacks include potential intrusiveness and the time-consuming effort required to reach many households, not to mention the emotional endurance required to face rejection repeatedly. The effectiveness of door-to-door sales depends on factors such as the product, the salesperson's skills, and cultural acceptance in the area. Security systems, solar panels, books, students and their sob stories, and window washing tend to work well. Here are a few examples of how I've personally seen door-to-door sales be effective for some businesses:

When I worked at a retail place back in the day, this guy came in asking a price of five times the minimum wage to clean our three big window panels. As a retail store, we needed clean windows, so we hired him. He did a good job, and with his tools, he was done in five minutes! He could probably have hit a dozen stores in an hour! That man was making good money.

In story number two, my wife was approached by some foreign college students during the summer of one year. They asked if she wanted to buy the book they were selling. When she said no, they asked if she had a room she'd be willing to rent while they were selling in the nearby area. She said no, but later that day, while I was on a walk with her, we decided it might be rather fun, so when we ran across him knocking on doors in a nearby neighborhood on our walk, we settled on a price, and he and his friends all lived at our house for the summer. They were gone by seven in the morning and didn't get back til around nine or later at night. Honestly, we hardly ever saw them.

There were different rotations of these foreign students who would come, and some I saw leave before their contracts were up because they just couldn't take the door-to-door lifestyle. But because the first guy asked, he allowed us to respond positively. The main principle behind door-to-door is you never know unless you ask.

As another example, one of my friends has a power washing business perfect for door-to-door sales. He goes to businesses and shows them how they need him, then gets them on a monthly contract. To start that business, you would only need a power washer. You could likely make that money back by the first contract's completion.

As far as personal experience goes, I sold Fuller Brush door-to-door. It was difficult for me. I did sell, but it was hard work. I didn't do it for long because it takes a certain type of person to sell door-to-door, and that was not me. For my lawn mowing and snowplow business, door-to-door was a great strategy. For selling things instead of a service, I realized it was not my desired method to make money. However, if you are good at it and can face the hardship, it does make good money.

Affiliate Marketing

Affiliate marketing is where you promote other people's products online and earn a commission for every sale or lead you generate. It's a performance-based marketing model, meaning you only get paid when you successfully promote and sell a product.

There are three types of affiliate marketing: unattached, related, and involved. Each of these affiliate methods has advantages and disadvantages, so conduct research beforehand.

Unattached: you simply share affiliate links without a personal connection to the product.

Related: you promote products related to your own content or niche.

Involved: you have a personal connection or experience with the product you're promoting.

For example, if you have a cooking blog, you might share an affiliate link for a popular kitchen gadget. You will earn a commission if your readers buy it through your link. A kitchen gadget on a cooking blog would sell better than a link for a lawn mower.

Final Thoughts

Thank you for joining me on this journey into the world of entrepreneurship. As we wrap up, I want to express my appreciation for your time. This book isn't just about stories or good ideas; hopefully, it is a lesson to help you start your own story.

As you enter the business world armed with new knowledge, remember that entrepreneurship is more than just making money. Keep what is important to you as your priority, and you will find a way for the rest of it to work out.

I hope you dream big, take calculated risks, and realize your entrepreneurial dreams. Thank you for being part of this journey. Here's to your boundless entrepreneurial spirit and the exciting possibilities ahead!

Find more tips and a community of aspiring entrepreneurs on our social media and websites! You can find us on our website at anyonecanstartabusiness.com for blogs and other resources or find us on social media at @anyonecanstartabusiness on Instagram, Facebook, and YouTube.

Notes

Notes

www.ingramcontent.com/pod-product-compliance
Lightning Source LLC
Chambersburg PA
CBHW062117080426
42734CB00012B/2892